AMERICAN CIRCUMSTANCE

Social Fictions Series

Series Editor
Patricia Leavy
USA

The *Social Fictions* series emerges out of the arts-based research movement. The series includes full-length fiction books that are informed by social research but written in a literary/artistic form (novels, plays, and short story collections). Believing there is much to learn through fiction, the series only includes works written entirely in the literary medium adapted. Each book includes an academic introduction that explains the research and teaching that informs the book as well as how the book can be used in college courses. The books are underscored with social science or other scholarly perspectives and intended to be relevant to the lives of college students—to tap into important issues in the unique ways that artistic or literary forms can.

Please email queries to pleavy7@aol.com

International Editorial Advisory Board

Carl Bagley, University of Durham, UK
Anna Banks, University of Idaho, USA
Carolyn Ellis, University of South Florida, USA
Rita Irwin, University of British Columbia, Canada
J. Gary Knowles, University of Toronto, Canada
Laurel Richardson, The Ohio State University (Emeritus), USA

American Circumstance

By

Patricia Leavy

SENSE PUBLISHERS
ROTTERDAM / BOSTON / TAIPEI

A C.I.P. record for this book is available from the Library of Congress.

ISBN 978-94-6209-285-3 (paperback)
ISBN 978-94-6209-286-0 (hardback)
ISBN 978-94-6209-287-7 (e-book)

Published by: Sense Publishers,
P.O. Box 21858, 3001 AW Rotterdam, The Netherlands
https://www.sensepublishers.com/

Printed on acid-free paper

DEDICATION

this book is a love letter to the people I grew up with,
and the man I want to grow old with, Mark Robins

TABLE OF CONTENTS

ACKNOWLEDGMENTS

First and foremost, thank you to publisher extraordinaire Peter de Liefde for your willingness to innovate and support creative projects. Thrilled to be working with you. Thank you to the entire Sense Publishers team. In particular, Bernice Kelly for your production assistance and Paul Chambers for all you do to market the Social Fictions series. My deepest appreciation to Gioia Chilton for creating the beautiful cover art. You are so talented! To the trailblazers on the Social Fictions editorial board—Carl Bagley, Anna Banks, Carolyn Ellis, Rita Irwin, J. Gary Knowles and Laurel Richardson—thank you for supporting the series. A huge shout-out to the world's best assistant, Shalen Lowell, who does more than can be covered here. I appreciate it all. I am deeply grateful to my Kennebunk writing group—David, Mort, Ning, Celine and Alan. Your support, helpful comments and friendship have fuelled this project. A most heartfelt thank you to my weekly writing buddy, Celine Boyle. Celine, you are a profoundly talented writer and exceptional friend. Your detailed, thoughtful and wise comments on every page of this manuscript, and your enthusiasm, made this a better book and made me a better writer. You are such a blessing in my life! Tori Amos, my musical muse—as you said, I too feel we are "kindred spirits" and I hope you see your influence on every page. Thank you for creating a model for female artists to realize their vision and retain creative control over their work. As always, hugs to the best in-laws one could hope for, Carolyn and Charles Robins. Ally Field, the thing we have done the longest is being one another's friend—hope we can always say that. Mr. Shuman, thank you for introducing me to the power of novels. Madeline, I love you more than all the words—you are so special. Finally, this book is a love letter to the people I grew up with, hope you know who you are, and the man I want to grow old with. Mark, I see who you are and I know how fortunate I am to have you, my great love.

PREFACE

Paige Michaels comes from the kind of wealth that few experience. The daughter of a notoriously successful banker who wielded great political power, she grew up in an extraordinary world peopled by the political leaders of tomorrow. A distant relationship with her mother, the ultimate hostess, also plays a significant role in her identity. Now a wife, mother and full-time supporter of an international women's organization, her life appears charmed to all those looking. But one mistake rooted in her past is threatening to unravel her perfect life. Paige's story intersects with the narratives of two of her friends. After years as a stay-at-home mother living in New Jersey, Mollie Johnston convinces her husband, Paul, to move back to New York, to fulfill her dream of living amid the bright lights. Mollie is uncomfortable in her own body and always worried about how others see her and Paul. Once she sees how the other half lives, will she come to see herself and her marriage more clearly? Gwen McAndrews is the ultimate New York socialite, and the envy of those impressed by her grandeur, but is there more than meets the eye? In addition to Paige, Mollie and Gwen, a cast of characters' stories are interwoven into the text—parents, children, care-takers, childhood friends, old lovers and spouses—showing how they all shape each other's stories.

   While written in a fun, chick-lit style, *American Circumstance* is a subversive novel about appearance versus reality; how people's lives and relationships look to others versus how they are experienced, and the complex ways that social class shapes identity and relationships, including the codes that guide the ways that we interact with each other. The themes of appearance versus reality and social class are interlinked in the pages that follow, as they are in life. *American Circumstance* provides a window into the replication of wealth, power and privilege. There is also a strong generational narrative about how family influences identity as well as a narrative about the power of friendship.

American Circumstance also explores the intersections between gender and class and how they shape identity and relationships in complicated ways. This is a wholly "American" story set in the Northeast. However, through Paige's work with WIN, an international organization devoted to helping women living in conflict and high-risk zones, we see that problems are all relative, as are the ways that race, class and gender influence our stories. (WIN is a fictitious organization inspired by the real organization Women for Women International. If you are interested in helping women in conflict zones please visit http://www.womenforwomen.org/.) *American Circumstance* also touches on sexual violence. If you or someone you know needs help please go to RAINN (the Rape, Abuse and Incest National Network, http://www.rainn.org/).

In order to push on the bounds of the appearance versus reality theme I conceptualized the novel as if it were an impressionist painting. An impressionist painting can look very different from a distance than close-up, much like our lives and relationships. There is a literary style that developed from the theory of impressionism. This approach to writing is based on associations, repetition and symbolism. In an effort to capture the impressionistic style I have employed particular writing strategies. Language is repeated in different contexts and shown to have a multiplicity of meanings, and details are included to evoke associations which may later be troubled. The novel is divided into three parts with the first (the longest) covering moments over an expanse of four decades. The second part unfolds over a period of a few months and the final part transpires over just a few days. A narrator's viewpoint dominates the beginning of the novel—providing a distant view—and the interiority of characters is increasingly presented as we reach the book's conclusion—providing a close-up perspective. In this regard the novel explores how others see the characters, how we as readers see them, and how they see themselves. As our perspective changes, and the characters and their circumstances are revealed, we are invited to consider what is truly important in their lives and hopefully in our own. This mirrors the practice of painting one scene at different angles, times of day or seasons, common in impressionist painting.

While entirely fictional, *American Circumstance* is grounded in autoethnographic observations (analyzed personal experiences) and more than a decade of teaching and sociological research about gender, class, race, identity and relationships. Fiction is a wonderful pedagogical tool and can be used to stimulate reflection and discussion about topics that are often challenging, such as social class. Sociology is concerned with the relationship between our individual lives and the larger contexts in which we live our lives. I used this perspective to weave a narrative about how social class and gender influence our life experiences, even the seemingly mundane, such as the way we interact with each other, often slipping into patterned or coded ways of communicating. I hope in doing so readers will be able to make connections between our societal environments and our individual lives. For me, *American Circumstance* is a pure a/r/tographical rendering—that which fully merges my artist-researcher-teacher identities. During the writing process I felt it was the book I was always meant to write. The novel can be used as supplemental reading in courses across the disciplines that deal with gender, social class, power, family systems, intimate relationships and/or identity, or it can be read entirely for pleasure.

Patricia Leavy

Part One

CHAPTER 1

Paige went down to the lobby to check the mail for the third time that morning. She had already checked both before and after her daily run, although she knew it was too early. Always rational, she justified this irrational behavior by lamenting that Saturday deliveries were unpredictable, and since the wait from Saturday to Monday was the worst she might as well check, and possibly calm herself. As she turned the tiny key and lifted the metal latch she wondered how much longer she could endure this. Still nothing. As she passed through the lobby again, she waved at the doorman, Frank, and scurried back into her elevator eager to return to the warmth of her home. Although already into April the last blizzard had blanketed New York with a coldness that had yet to pass. Her slim frame couldn't let go of the chill. She rubbed her hands together wondering if her trembling was from the cold, anxiety or guilt. *What kind of mother am I?* played over and over in her mind.

Not wanting to keep her friend Gwen waiting she darted up to third floor of the penthouse, slipped on her boots and darted into her bathroom removing a hair tie from a drawer. She took her brush and pulled her long dark auburn hair tightly into a high ponytail, making certain to smooth any flyaway strands. She uncharacteristically indulged for a moment searching the reflection for someone familiar. As she looked in the large bathroom mirror perfecting her hair she wondered where she had disappeared to. Then, remembering she was meeting Gwen she shook her head and lunged back into her routine. She grabbed her workout bag and scoured her walk-in closet for her handbag until she remembered leaving it by the front door, to save time. She hurried downstairs, threw the handbag into her workout bag and put on her Burberry coat. She cinched the belt tightly as if to confirm that she was in fact there. In an effort to hide in public she grabbed a pair of oversized black Chanel sunglasses from her mail table, slipped them on and left.

Upon arrival at the health club she made a beeline to the locker room whizzing past a woman she didn't think she knew. As she brushed past on route to her locker the woman called after her, "Paige? Paige Michaels, is that you?"

Paige turned around too flustered to recognize her at first. She was beaming with an out-of-place friendliness. Her round face and dark blonde curls seemed familiar but the fullness of her face suggested she was overweight and not pumped up with Botox so Paige couldn't quite place her.

"It's me, Mollie Johnston! Well, Mollie Cooper back then but now…"

As recognition set in Paige interrupted with, "Oh, oh hi Mollie," catching her breath and slowly backtracking towards the jolly woman.

"Well you're practically incognito aren't you?" Mollie remarked with a bright smile.

Paige took off her sunglasses and leaned in to peck Mollie on the cheek. "I'm so sorry. I'm running late for my squash game… Wow. It has been ages," Paige continued, finally in control of her breathing.

"Since college. Well you look just wonderful, put together as ever. Still just perfect. Perfect Paige just as always. I'm jealous!" she said as she gave Paige the once over. "I've been on the waitlist for this place for ages. I'm so glad to see a friendly face," Mollie continued.

"It's nice to see you too," Paige replied in a concerted effort to appear friendly. She could see that Mollie meant well but she wasn't in the mood to smile through awkwardly worded compliments. "So, you live in the city now?" she continued out of courtesy.

"Yes, yes just about fifteen blocks from here. My husband, you remember Paul?" Paige smiled ever so slightly in confirmation, and Mollie continued, "Paul's at a big firm in Midtown and the boys started college last year, one is at Bates and the other at Colby, so I have a lot more time to myself—we have twin boys, gosh did I even tell you that?" Without waiting for a reply Mollie continued, "Anyway, you can see why I was so desperate for a space to open here! So, what about you? Don't tell me, you're blissfully happy with Spencer of course—what about kids, do you have any kids?"

"Mollie I don't mean to be rude but I'm terribly late for my match. It's wonderful seeing you. Let's catch up another time," Paige said, already backing away.

"Oh gosh, I didn't mean to hold you up," Mollie replied in a jovial tone. Paige was already walking away but put her hand up in a backward wave as Mollie hollered, "Great seeing you!"

With her back to Mollie and several yards away Paige nodded, one perfect loose curl of her ponytail bouncing up and down as she continued to walk away.

After changing into her all-whites and re-stocking her locker with a stack of freshly pressed clothes she met Gwen who was already warming up on the court. As Paige opened the glass door, the always-glamorous Gwen turned around and said, "I can't believe I finally beat you here. It only took three years. Do you want to warm-up?"

"I was cornered in the locker room. Let's go, your serve."

*

After showering and getting dressed Paige sat in front of the locker room makeup mirror tightening her ponytail as Gwen, seated next to her, complained about the fine lines fanning out from her eyes.

"I mean honestly Paige, they're getting worse," she said as she brushed at them with her fingers, as if to rub them away. "I don't know how this happened so quickly. It's dreadful. I religiously use that serum and for hundreds for a tiny little tube, god you'd think I'd look better than this. If that stuff doesn't work it's hopeless."

Paige was now applying her sheer pink lip gloss while Gwen continued, "I think I should get a consultation. I mean if I'm going to do something, better to do it before it interferes with summer travel. Sometimes you can't have any sun exposure for ages and we're heading to Capri. And you know recovery is always longer than they say. What do you think?" she asked, now laughing as she turned her head and tightly pulled the skin near her eyes.

5

Paige smiled and waved her lip gloss wand at her saying, "Don't be silly, you look fabulous, I can hardly see a thing. If you start now, you know what will happen. You'll have to keep going and eventually you'll look like Barbara, the poor dear."

Before Gwen could respond a shadow dimmed the bright makeup mirror lights, and they realized they were not alone.

"Oh, hi Mollie," Paige said, turning on her stool. "Mollie, this is my friend Gwen McAndrews." As the women smiled at each other Paige continued, "Mollie and I went to Columbia together. She just joined."

"Oh, how nice," Gwen said. "Have you lived in the city long?"

"We recently moved back, my husband and boys and I. We were living in New Jersey. In East Brunswick, do you know it?" Mollie rambled.

Gwen smiled although she found Mollie oddly chatty.

"Mollie is married to a wonderful man," Paige interjected. "He was always, always so solid, so dependable. I'm sure he's a terrific father."

Mollie was overcome by the compliment, especially coming from Paige who in college would never have given a guy like Paul the time of day. Mollie always assumed Paige looked at him as plain, common.

"Yes, Paul is wonderful. In fact we moved back into the city because he knew how I missed it and with the boys in college…" Mollie continued, beaming.

But before she could finish Gwen stood up and said, "We're heading to La Rue for our post-game brunch. You should join us." Gwen was an expert at spotting the money-set, and she knew this pudgy, rosy cheeked woman was not a part of it, but Paige knew her, and so she wanted to be polite. Gwen was curious too, as Mollie seemed so obviously out of her element.

Paige had the best poker face of anyone Gwen had ever known. In fact, she used to tease Paige that she could be a spy in the CIA, but she did have one tell. When unpleasantly surprised, Paige reactively blinked her eyes. While Mollie never would have noticed,

6

Gwen saw how her invitation caused this involuntary reaction from Paige and she became all the more intrigued.

"Oh, I wouldn't want to intrude," Mollie said in a way that made it clear she very much wanted to join the women.

"Nonsense," Paige said, standing up and cinching the belt on her coat, please join us."

With that Paige and Gwen flung their bags over their shoulders and the three women headed out.

*

"Hi, Hon," Paul said as Mollie entered their small apartment. "So is the health club all you imagined?" he asked as he turned the page in the newspaper he was reading. Mollie put her bag down by the door, locked the double lock and walked into their galley kitchen. Paul remained sitting at the round table in the one small common room.

"Well, you won't believe who I saw," Mollie said as she drew a glass of water from the tap. "Paige Michaels."

"Wow, that's a blast from the past," Paul said, folding over the corner of the newspaper to peer over at his wife. "How is she?"

"She's wonderful. She hasn't changed a bit," Mollie said, stopping to sip her water. "She's as gorgeous and put together as ever. She introduced me to one of her friends and they actually invited me to lunch. We went to this member's only club which was as Chi-Chi as you can imagine. They had to sign me in as their guest. All the food was so pretty it was hard to eat it. My plate looked like art. Of course they have "regular" orders and aren't even given menus—Paige gets two poached eggs with one slice of tomato and one slice of turkey bacon. Isn't that weird? She goes to this amazing place every week and has the same thing, and it's something so boring, and it isn't even a normal size order—they just bring it to her. Her friend has a lobster Cobb salad. Have you ever even heard of such a thing? She said she had one in Maine on vacation and now the restaurant makes it especially for her. Amazing."

"Uh huh, well that sounds nice," Paul said, now reading his paper again.

"You should have seen Paige, and Gwen, Paige's friend Gwen…"

"Uh huh."

"They…" and then Mollie searched for the words. "They look like they stepped off of a movie screen or magazine cover or something. Everything is just as it should be, down to their perfect hair. I mean perfect, not a stray strand anywhere. Gwen's hair looks just like Marilyn Monroe. And the parties they go to— big galas at museums and opera houses. The mayor was at an event they attended last weekend and he sat at Paige's table! Can you believe it?"

"Didn't Paige always run with that kind of crowd? Her father was that famous banker slash fat-cat, um, John Michaels, right?" Paul asked from behind his newspaper.

"Yeah, I guess. Anyway, maybe we'll get invited to something like that," Mollie said.

"Well I'm glad you're happy and that you have some friends," Paul said. He remembered Paige from college and found her boring and didn't see why Mollie admired her so, but as always, he only wanted Mollie's happiness. Paul had never known truly intense passion until he met her, and over the years that only grew. Despite her insecurities, Mollie was able to be free with him and her vulnerability was intoxicating. There was nothing he wouldn't do for her. He had given up his comfortable suburban life for a dingy four-floor walk-up in which he and Mollie were practically on top of each other. He knew Mollie dreamt of being in the city and so he made the move although he couldn't afford to replicate their suburban life in the city (nor could he afford any of the luxuries Mollie wanted, like the ultra-exclusive health club membership). But she was willing to skimp on everything else, even clipping coupons for groceries just to have two things: an apartment in Manhattan and a membership to that health club (for which she had been waitlisted for more than a year). He knew that Mollie wasn't a social climber or even particularly interested in material things, it was just that she had dreamt of a bigger life than she had lived. All of those years in New Jersey as a stay-at-home wife and mother she had thought of the sparkling lights on the other side of the Hudson. For years she dreamt of the life of the artists who lived there. As time passed she began thinking about the women she went to college with, who were living lives she only saw on television. Once her sons were grown and going to college she asked Paul to move into the city and, knowing all he needed for happiness was her, he didn't hesitate to give in to her request.

*

When Paige arrived home she again stopped at the mailbox, but it was empty. She entered her triple decker Park Avenue penthouse and walked into the kitchen where she was greeted by her housekeeper Gert, who offered to make her a post-workout smoothie. "No thanks, Gert, but please bring a pot of coffee to my office. I am going to work. Please ask Chloe to come see me when she gets home."

Paige locked herself in her office for the next several hours working on the plans for a charity event she was hosting to raise money for breast cancer research. Although she was far more committed to her global outreach work for women in impoverished countries, which had become her life's work, she had taken up the cause of breast cancer a year earlier after her mother passed away from the disease. Although they had never been close, as no one could be close to Eleanor, Paige felt it was the right thing to do. There was also an irony not lost on her. Paige's mother had been the ultimate hostess, which growing up Paige looked down on as trivial. Now Paige, who put her double degree in art history and international studies in service of a life of charitable party planning, was finally hosting a gala in honor of her mother. Eleanor—whose wit was greater than Paige knew as a child, would have loved it.

Late afternoon there was a knock on the office door.

"Yes," Paige said softly, immersed in party details.

"Hey, Mom," Chloe said as she entered the room.

"How was your match?" Paige asked as she turned around to give Chloe her attention.

"We put up a good fight but alas, it was not to be."

Paige smiled. "Well, maybe next time. What else is going on?"

"I hung out with Chelsea for a while. She just broke up with some guy and needed girl-time."

"Oh, well that's nice of you," Paige said. "What are you doing tonight? Any plans or are you having dinner at home? Dad and I have an event but I can ask Gert to fix you something"

"I'm going to a movie with Chris and then Chelsea asked me to crash at her place. Is that Ok?"

"Sure. Have a good time but make sure you're back in time for your fitting tomorrow. The seamstress is coming by at noon."

"Fitting for what?" Chloe asked, puzzled.

"The dress for the gala, remember? I told you I picked up the champagne Stella McCartney you wanted but it has to be fitted."

"Oh, right. I'll be back in time. Besides, it's not for like ages."

"Please don't say like. I'm trying to plan ahead and stay on top of things."

"Ok," Chloe said.

"Well, have a good time. And don't let Chelsea eat too much junk—break-ups can really wreck a girl's will."

Chloe giggled—unable to imagine anything interfering with her mother's willpower. As Chloe started to leave the room Paige, now facing her computer, softly asked, "Oh Chloe, any word from Stanford yet?"

"Nope," she said as she casually walked out of the room, shutting the door behind her.

Paige held her breath and shut her eyes for a moment before resuming her work.

CHAPTER 2

As a girl Paige's life had always seemed terribly ordinary to her, but to anyone else looking in, it was anything but. Paige came from the kind of wealth that few could ever understand. It was the kind of wealth that had always been there and would always be there. No economic meltdown or new innovation threatened their security or lifestyle, it was as dependable as the sunrise. With this level of reliability and normalcy came the threat of entitlement and this was something she witnessed many times in the homes of her nearly equally fortunate friends. However, Paige seemed to float above it and eventually her curiosity and compassion provided her the purpose in life that held entitlement at bay. She lived in this extraordinary world as if it were ordinary, and to her it quite genuinely was.

Paige spent the school year in her family Estate in Wellesley, Massachusetts. It had been in her family for generations. Everything about the estate screamed New England money and gave away her secretly extraordinary life to those invited into its sanctuary. The house was great fun to any child with the slightest imagination. There were secret passageways, multiple stairway escapes from any given spot in the house (often used to escape the nanny at bath time and bedtime), and walk-in closets that Paige played in for hours. She also loved the view from her bedroom windows onto the large Weeping Willows in the backyard. As a child she thought they looked as soft as flowing cotton candy and still remembers with disappointment the day she reached up and touched a hanging leaf to discover it felt just the same as the leaves on all the other trees. That was her first taste of bitter sweetness.

Although the house was fully staffed with housekeepers, nannies, a driver and an on-call chef, Paige always refused to be driven to school, she preferred taking the school bus, she claimed, so that she could ride along with the other children. She made this clear at the age of five.

On her first day of kindergarten her parents stood by the front door with her waiting while her nanny, Agnes, ran to the kitchen to

11

get her lunchbox. Her mother, Eleanor, leaned down and straightened the white collar of her shirt and then ran her hands down the front of her skirt, to flatten any creases, although it had already been pressed perfectly. She gave her a peck on the forehead and said, "Have a lovely day." Then, her father, who made sure to be home for this momentous occasion, leaned down and said, "Go get 'em. And remember, Daddy loves you." At that moment Agnes delivered Paige her Wonder Woman lunchbox and said, "I will walk you to the car."

"Oh no, I am going to take the bus Aggie."

Agnes looked stunned and looked over at Paige's parents. Her father chuckled. Eleanor on the other hand looked perturbed. She leaned down and said, "Henry will take you to school dear, that's his job. Now you don't want to be late."

Paige shook her head and repeated, "No. I am taking the bus. I want to ride the big yellow bus with the other children."

Eleanor, looking agitated, opened her mouth to say something at which point John laughed even louder and said, "Well that's my girl isn't it?" He patted Paige on the head and directed Agnes to get his phonebook. Moments later he was on the phone, with his back turned and mumbling something Paige couldn't understand. Eleanor stood as still as a statue until her husband turned around.

"It will be fine, Ellie," he said, looking at his wife whose face held expressionless dismay. He then turned his attention to Paige and said, "All right Paige. The school bus will pick you up and drop you off at the bottom of the drive. You best hurry, they're making a special trip to come and get you." He then turned to Agnes and said, "Please see her safely on and off the bus."

"Yes, Sir," Agnes replied.

"I don't need Aggie to take me Daddy, I can do it by myself," Paige said, looking up at her father, in whose eyes she saw the whole world sparkling back at her.

"Aggie will see you on and off the bus. That's the deal, Ok?"

"Ok, Daddy."

And with that began the ritual Paige continued through high school, much to the dismay of her mother who never again saw her off in the morning. By the age of six Paige had convinced her father to let her walk up and down the path on her own. Although she adored Aggie and missed their chats she relished the independence. Riding with the other children had never been her goal. Paige enjoyed meandering down the road, looking up, at times quite uncharacteristically tripping over her own feet. The private road leading to their sprawling seven-bedroom and ten-bath home was lined with pine trees so high they covered the sky. Sometimes big black cars with tinted windows drove past, *important men meeting Daddy* she assumed. She paid them no mind, and just walked, watching the trees trying to find the sky. For someone remarkably regimented, it was the only time she really slowed down and it was for this reason she always insisted on taking the bus. It wasn't until a child sitting on the bus told her that the bus had changed its route to pick her up at the bottom of her private drive that Paige realized her father must have done something quite special to get the school bus there, particularly on that first morning—which at the time seemed normal to her. This thought made her smile, not because she liked the idea that her father could always get people to do very special things, but because when he did it was usually for her.

Summers were split evenly between their beach-front homes in Kennebunkport, Maine and Chatham on Cape Cod. The magnificent estates with wrap-around porches overlooking the Atlantic were almost indiscernible from one another except the porch in Kennebunkport was lined with white Adirondack chairs and the house in Chatham was lined with dark green lounge chairs. The small things differed, and these were what she noticed and remembered.

For example, the path to the beach in Maine was lined with green bushes on each side with bright pink Rugosa roses popping against the blue water and sky. In Cape Cod, the pathway, similarly long and winding was marked with long flowing grass on either side. The only difference in the beach experience itself was whether her view included Maine's famous rocky coast or the Cape's endangered sand dunes. Aggie took her to the beach everyday weather permitted, so she got to know the views quite well. Like everything else in Paige's life, there was a predictable routine. Paige always wore a brightly colored swimsuit with matching skirt and accessories. Her favorite was a bright aqua one piece suit with a crisscross back for which she had a matching hat and sunglasses. Aggie carried their chairs, an umbrella and a small cooler packed with sandwiches and bottled water. Paige carried two towels and a beach bag filled with books, sand toys and ultra-strong sunscreen her mother insisted on. They sat together, collected shells, made castles, ate sandwiches (Paige loved peanut butter and jelly best of all but her mother usually made Agnes pack turkey rollups) and splashed around in the freezing water.

Other than spending long days at the beach Paige's summers consisted of private tennis lessons (wearing whites only), daily sessions with a tutor that her mother insisted on (she was to learn French although she didn't know why) and lots of visits from family friends and her father's business associates (which required her to sit, politely, and listen to adult conversation). Her parents often hosted large outdoor cookouts. She loved the way the staff hung white twinkling lights on the trees and transformed the backyard into someplace magical with round tables draped in tulle and covered with little candles. With the strong scent of pine in the air it felt like where the Sugar Plum fairies might live. While her mother was always too busy socializing to talk to Paige, her father often pulled her to his side and rubbed the top of her head as he talked about business and politics to the hamburger-eating men that stood in a circle around him. No matter who was there she was struck by how everyone seemed to hang on every word her father said. They seemed to like to be near him almost as much as she did. It wasn't until she was nine that she realized her father wasn't just a regular businessman.

They were invited to a Fourth of July clambake at the Kennedy compound in Hyannis Port. Paige was excited when they pulled up to the security gate at the Kennedy estate and her father showed his ID. The guard said, "Of course Mr. Michaels, you're expected." *Everyone*, she thought, *knows Daddy*. At the clambake she watched him huddled in a corner with Ted Kennedy and two other men she had seen on television.

In August they were invited to an end-of summer cookout at the Bush residence on Walker Point—a private peninsula jutting out from Kennebunkport. When she asked her mother who the Bushes were, Eleanor replied, "Remember the Kennedys? Well one day the Bushes will be the Kennedys, but in red ties dear."

"How do you know they'll be like that, Mom?"

"Because Daddy and his friends said so."

Well-known politicians had been in and out of their doors for as long as she could remember, but now at an age where she understood more about politics, the events of the summer struck her. It wasn't until the end of that summer when they were attending the Bush cook-out that Paige realized her father was an important man. He was somehow beyond the politics of any one party and yet needed by them all. After the cook-out she went into her mother's powder room as she sat in front of her vanity removing her earrings. Paige asked, "How come we were invited to the cook-out?"

"Because your father is friends with the family," she said, never making eye contact.

"But how is Daddy friends with them?"

"Through business," Eleanor replied, now removing her eye makeup.

"What exactly does Daddy do?" Paige asked.

"He's a businessman, you know that."

"But what does he make?"

Eleanor smiled and turned to Paige, "He makes money, sweetheart."

"Well I know he makes money. But how does he make money? Does he make anything else?"

Eleanor paused and then turned to Paige and smirked, which was the closest she ever came to smiling. "Power. Daddy makes money by making power."

"How do you make power?" she asked, confused.

"You go to clambakes at the Kennedy's and cook-outs at the Bush's. Now run off to bed."

*

15

Paige's life continued without deviation for years during which she learned the values of discipline and control from her mother, and charity from her father. Although she always knew she was a "Daddy's girl," she greatly admired her mother's dignity and elegance. Eleanor was in complete control—never uttering an unintended word or raising her voice. Her days were organized like folders in a filing cabinet—punctuated with her daily exercise routine and strictly adhered to diet which, no doubt, were responsible for her never-changing slim figure. Not only was she always dressed impeccably for every situation, but even more so she quite literally looked perfect, making those around her seem like flawed mortals. Once when Paige was eleven she and her mother accompanied her father on a business trip to Chicago. It was the only time her mother didn't bring Agnes to watch her. Instead, Eleanor took Paige to The Art Institute of Chicago. She led her to the post-impressionist room and they stood in front of George Seurat's *Seated Woman with a Parasol*. Eleanor put her hand on Paige's shoulder and said, "This is my favorite painting. What do you think?"

Paige wanted to say the right thing so she thought carefully for a moment and then replied, "I love it."

There was a silence and Paige looked more closely at the painting. Then, she turned and looked at her mother and said, "She's very graceful, and yet she's sitting up straight and strong. I wonder what she's looking for... I think it reminds me of you, Mom."

Eleanor's eyes brightened, she squeezed Paige's shoulder, and they continued their tour of the museum.

To Paige, Eleanor epitomized the values of discipline and grace and Paige worked hard to emulate her.

By the time she was thirteen she woke up every morning by 6 am to go for a 3 mile run. She loved the way running allowed her to clear her mind and just go. Running, coupled with her strict no-frills diet, gave her a washboard body. She exceled in school consistently earning perfect GPAs, and she filled every moment of her afternoons with homework, track and tennis, piano and ballet lessons. Fascinated with art, she wanted to take pottery classes but her mother didn't allow her to—the clay was too messy. Reliably occupied, organized and controlled, Paige simply accepted her mother's decision and carried on. Paige believed every spare minute should be used and so she continually added "acceptable" activities and interests to her already-impressive repertoire. As she got older her father tried to teach her the importance of giving back. During her junior year in high school she began tutoring the underprivileged kids who were bussed into her private school on scholarships. It was this simple addition to her schedule that caused her life to change, and for the first time, for Paige to knowingly experience something extraordinary.

CHAPTER 3

Paige was assigned to tutor freshman Kayla Washington. On the first day of the program all of the tutors were scheduled to meet the kids in the cafeteria before school, to have breakfast together and get to know each other. Paige learned that these kids were dropped off 45 minutes before classes began each day, because most were on special meal plans that allowed for a free or nearly free breakfast. As Paige stood in a row with her fellow tutors, eagerly waiting for the 'underprivileged' kids to arrive, she overheard two guys to her right talking about how the whole bussing program was bullshit but they knew their participation would look good on college applications. Paige knew these guys from class, and their college applications would need all the help they could get. If they weren't legacy kids she thought they'd be lucky to get into a community college. When one of the guys said, "If they can't cut it here, then they shouldn't come," Paige opened her mouth to say something but never got the chance. At that moment a group of kids she had never seen before came into the room. The quiet was filled with chatter as backpacks were flung to the floor, and kids tried to figure out who they were partnered with. Suddenly there was a short, very dark-skinned African-American girl standing in front of her. Paige smiled but before she could say something the girl said, "You're Paige, right? I'm Kayla, but everyone calls me Kay-Kay, Ok?" The girl laughed at the sound of "Kay-Kay, Ok" which Paige suspected never ceased to cause a giggle. There was something incredibly infectious about her. Paige liked her immediately.

"It's so nice to meet you, Kayla," Paige said, outstretching her arm to shake her hand.

"Kay-Kay, call me Kay-Kay," she replied. "The line is getting long, let's get in it. I'm starving."

"Oh, I already ate actually, but you go ahead while I get seats for us."

"It's free ya know," she said in disbelief. "They're payin for it so we can get to know each other and stuff. And let me tell you, a free meal doesn't come by every day. Come on," she said as she took

Paige's hand and walked her to the back of the line. Paige took an orange juice and an apple to be polite. Kay-Kay loaded her tray with two boxes of Rice Krispies, milk, orange juice, a banana and a bagel. Paige wondered how such a small girl could eat so much.

They sat at one end of a long cafeteria table and as they ate Kay-Kay told Paige that she was a good student and worked hard but sometimes the teachers didn't like what she wrote. She also told Paige about her life (she lived with her mother and younger brother in an area of Boston Paige had never been to but perceived as "bad"), her aspirations (she wanted to be a fashion designer and own a chain of stores), and her views on the school (she liked getting out of her neighborhood and felt lucky to go to the school but didn't think all of her teachers "got" her). She especially liked getting out of her apartment since her mother worked out of their home, as a telemarketer. School provided much needed space. She talked the whole time, with great energy and excitement, pausing only to eat her cereal. Paige asked why she had never seen her before and learned that she had been placed in remedial level classes that were held in a different part of the school.

"Don't ya know, that's where they put us to start, but we can place out."

Paige, never one to reveal much with her expressions, just took the information in causing Kay-Kay to continue explaining it to her. "You know, get into more advanced stuff. That's why I need you, to help me place out. I want to be in the good classes so I get into a good college. I want to go to FIT in New York, but I want to study business too, you know, so I can be in control."

As Paige continued processing this, Kay-Kay wrapped her bagel into a napkin and slid it into the front pouch of her backpack.

"Ok, so we have a goal—helping you place out. We should come up with a schedule. We are required to meet for at least three hours a week. What's good for you?" Paige asked.

"The bus drops me at 7:30 every morning so I have 45 minutes before classes start. I'm free most afternoons too, but I have to catch the late bus or I'm stuck."

"Why don't we meet in the mornings for now and see how it goes?" Paige asked. "But it's too loud in here. I would rather work with you in the library."

"Ok, meet me at the bus drop tomorrow at 7:30 and we can go to the library together," Kay-Kay said.

The next morning Paige was waiting at the bus drop at 7:20. She wanted to make sure she was on time so Kay-Kay would know she took the responsibility seriously. At exactly 7:30 the bus pulled up. Paige started scanning the passengers through the windows, looking for Kay-Kay. Her eyes moved slowly from the front of the bus down each window until she was nearly at the end when her head stopped at the sight of a guy who looked like he stepped off of the stage at a rock concert. He was tall and his muscular chest and arms seemed to be busting out of his clothes. He had creamy white skin, long silken brown hair nearly to his waist, and he was wearing a blue bandana that moments later, when he passed her, she realized matched his piercing eyes. On that bus, he was the ultimate misfit.

"Uh, hello, there," she suddenly heard as Kay-Kay waved her hand in front of Paige's face.

"Oh, hi Kay-Kay. How are you?"

"Girl, you sleepwalking or something? That's why you need to eat a good breakfast, for energy. I don't want my tutor falling asleep."

"Oh, no, I was... I was," but she was unusually tongue-tied. Then, from 20 feet away, a male voice yelled, "Kay-Kay, you owe me one."

Kay-Kay turned and giggled, as Paige looked to discover it was him. Catching Paige staring she said, "Ohhh, now I see what's got you, you and every other girl. You've never met Jake before."

"What, uh no, I was just..." Paige stammered.

"It's Ok girl, don't feel bad. He's fine and like every girl I know has a thing for him. Except me. Gross," Kay-Kay said as she started heading for the library, with Paige in tow.

"No, I was just surprised to, to..." but she didn't know how to finish.

"Surprised to see a white dude on a bus with all black kids, right?"

Before Paige could swallow her mortification to respond Kay-Kay continued, "Jake lives in the same apartment building I live in, you know, in the projects. We all give him shit about being the only white dude in the program, but he's a good guy, for a player."

"A player?"

"That dude has more girls going in and out of his place than a McDonald's drive-through."

A minute later the girls were entering the school library. They spent 40 minutes working on Kay-Kay's social studies project. When they finished Kay-Kay said, "It's supposed to be raining tomorrow. From now on I can just meet you in the library if you want."

"That's all right, I don't mind meeting you at the bus," Paige replied.

*

For the next four weeks Paige met Kay-Kay every morning. Each day she scanned the bus until she caught a glimpse of Jake. He seemed so out of place, and her curiosity was like a magnetic pull drawing her to him. But she only allowed herself a quick peek so that no one would notice, not even Kay-Kay. A couple of times she could swear he was trying to steal a glimpse of her too, but she wasn't sure.

During this time she became good friends with Kay-Kay and came to think of her like a little sister. In addition to their morning tutoring sessions, Paige started seeking Kay-Kay out at lunch and inviting her to sit with her friends. Kay-Kay was confident, upbeat, wickedly funny and never held back. When Paige's friend Laurel was contemplating getting a new hairstyle she asked the group what they thought. After a series of niceties like, "Oh, you'll look great no matter what you do," Kay-Kay shook her head and said, "Girl, you got a big forehead and you need to get some bangs. Don't get me wrong, you're beautiful, but you've gotta tone down that forehead." After a short pause the girls, including Laurel, burst into laughter. Then, one by one, the girls each said, "Yeah, it's true. Go for some bangs." The next day Laurel came to school with long side-swept bangs. Kay-Kay was officially in the group.

After working together in the mornings for a month, Kay-Kay asked Paige if for the next week she could tutor her after school at her apartment. Her mother was going out of town for a few days to deal with a family problem and Kay-Kay needed to take care of her brother, Trey. Kay-Kay needed to take the late bus to school and then had to race home to relieve the neighbor watching Trey. Paige agreed. She planned to finish her own afterschool activities and then head to Kay-Kay's in the late afternoon. They could do Kay-Kay's homework while Trey watched TV or played in the other room.

That Monday, Paige, who normally drove herself around, asked the family driver to take her to Kay-Kay's after school. She was afraid of getting lost in a bad neighborhood, and she didn't want to be roaming around alone. Kay-Kay told her to beep when she got there so she could meet her downstairs. As Paige stepped out of the back of the black town car, Kay-Kay said, "You come to the projects in a limo? A limo? What were you thinking? Well at least I don't have to introduce you to anyone. You just introduced yourself to the whole neighborhood! Ok, come on," she said, taking Paige's hand and leading her into the stucco building.

Paige followed Kay-Kay through the dark corridors lit with flickering florescent lighting strips running across the low ceiling. They entered a stairwell which was dank and smelled faintly of garbage. They went up one floor and walked down another corridor and arrived at Kay-Kay's front door. There were some people having a chat at the end of the hallway and they gawked a bit at the sight of a stranger. Paige smiled at them and followed Kay-Kay in. She was happy to find that the apartment was warm and filled with the scent of Kay-Kay's perfume. She casually scanned the place. The living room was in front of her and she immediately saw Trey, sitting on the floor and watching a cartoon. There was a galley kitchen to the right and what looked like more rooms to the left. The living room was rectangular with white walls plastered with family photos, several pieces of art and a framed travel poster. There were two overstuffed comfortable looking couches, a coffee table covered with toys, an over-stocked bookcase, a television sitting on top of a cabinet, and a desk in the far corner near one of the two windows. It was very homey. Paige wasn't sure what she had expected. She wondered what it was like to live there.

"Come here and meet Trey."

Paige walked over as Kay-Kay touched Trey's shoulder and said, "Meet my friend Paige." Trey turned around and looked past Paige. She knew immediately that he had special needs. Paige bent down and said, "It's so nice to meet you, Trey."

"Say it's nice to meet you too," Kay-Kay said to Trey.

Trey had already turned to face the television but mumbled something that sounded like "nice to meet you."

"You stay here and watch your show while Paige and I go do homework in my room. If you need something just come get me." Kay-Kay then turned to Paige and asked, "Do you want something to drink or a snack or something?"

"Oh, no thank you," Paige replied.

"Let's go to my room," Kay-Kay said as Paige followed her. Kay-Kay pointed and said, "That's my Mom's room, that's the bathroom, and here's my room. I share with Trey." Paige followed her in and was initially overcome by the chaos. As she took a breath to get her bearings she was struck by how much Kay-Kay had done to make her bedroom special. On the far side of the room the walls were covered with ads from fashion magazines as well as Kay-Kay's sketches. There was a desk with a hutch filled with drawing supplies. Kay-Kay's bed had a hot pink, neon green, black and white bed spread and several fluffy decorative pillows that reminded Paige of feather boas. The other side of the room had kids' pictures of airplanes, helicopters and trains. Trey's twin bed had a railroad-themed bedspread and lots of stuffed animals.

Noticing Paige checking-out the room, Kay-Kay said, "He's obsessed with anything that moves, as you can see. He likes wheels and propellers. You can sit on his bed while I get my stuff out."

As Paige sat down on the bed she said, "Trey is adorable. Does he… does he…" Kay-Kay, never missing a beat, interjected with, "He was diagnosed with autism when he was two. My mom

24

had been a legal secretary before that but she wanted to spend more time with Trey so she quit her job and started doing telemarketing from home. That's how we ended up here. We used to have a big apartment in Jamaica Plain, where I didn't have to share a room," Kay-Kay said with frustration as she whipped her social studies notebook out of the drawer in her desk.

"That's amazing that your mother did that. What about your father? Does he help?"

"My father left when Trey was a baby and we haven't seen him since. And yeah, my mother is Superwoman, and I love Trey to death but shit, look at his stuff in my room," Kay-Kay said, pointing to a toy helicopter lodged in between two fashion books on her desk.

The girls laughed and started on Kay-Kay's homework. Two hours later Kay-Kay had to make dinner for Trey, and Paige needed to get home. Kay-Kay offered to walk her downstairs but Paige told her to go ahead and get Trey his dinner. She hugged Kay-Kay, said goodbye to Trey and left the apartment. As she made her way to the stairwell an apartment door opened, and a blonde girl with way too much hairspray and flushed cheeks walked out, and headed for the stairs. As Paige passed by the apartment she saw Jake standing shirtless in the doorway. He looked even taller framed by the low ceiling and he had tattoos traveling up his arms. She did a double take and kept walking. He stepped out into the hallway and called after her, "You're not even going to say hi?"

She turned around and said, "Excuse me."

"Aw, you're gonna be like that are you? Like you have no idea who I am."

"I don't know who you are," Paige said snidely, slowly walking back towards him.

"Oh, Ok, play it like that," he said with a smile.

She shook her head and turned around.

"Missed you at the bus stop today," he hollered after her.

Paige again stopped and turned around. She walked over, smiled and put out her hand. "I'm Paige, Kay-Kay's friend."

He shook her hand and laughed. "Yeah, I know who you are. So where were you this morning?"

"I tutor Kay-Kay in the mornings but today we needed to meet after school." Feeling awkward she shook her head a bit and said, "Ok, I gotta go. It was nice to meet you, well, sort of."

"I'm Jake," he said firmly.

"Well nice to meet you, Jake, but I have to go. And you look like you could use a rest," she said with a smirk as she gave him a onceover.

He smiled and looked down sheepishly.

As Paige started walking away he again called after her, "So will you be at the bus stop tomorrow?"

"Not this week, meeting Kay-Kay after school." She shook her head in a self-deprecating way, wondering why she was telling him this.

"Good night. Stay safe. I'll look out the window and make sure you get off all right," he hollered.

She lifted up her arm and gave a backward wave just as she entered the stairwell. As her driver opened the car door she couldn't resist. She tried to casually turn and look up but there was nothing casual about it. Jake, still shirtless, was standing in the window and he waved. She pretended not to notice although the slightest smile crept across her face. When she got into her car Henry asked if she would need a ride the next day. "No, that's Ok. I think I'll take my own car."

*

The next day she walked slowly past Jake's apartment on her way to Kay-Kay's. She half expected him to pop out to see her, but he didn't. During their tutoring session Kay-Kay sensed Paige was distracted.

"Ok, what's up?" Kay-Kay asked as she shut her history book.

"What do you mean? Nothings up," Paige replied in her usual controlled manner.

"Are you daydreaming about a boy? Let me guess, some superstar jock? You probably go for those beefy, preppy-ass dudes, am I right?" she prodded.

In a hushed tone Paige replied, "Can I ask you something without you laughing at me or saying anything to anyone?"

"Yeah, of course."

Looking straight into Kay-Kay's eyes she asked, "What's the deal with that guy... Jake?"

"Oh no girl. Don't go down that road. Don't get me wrong, he's an awesome guy. In fact, his tough guy thing is all an act. He's watched Trey for me before and he always helps my mom take the garbage out. But that boy likes girls, *all* the girls, and they sure like him," she took a breath and continued, "It's those blue eyes, I guess." Then, turning more quizzical, Kay-Kay tilted her chin down and in an uncharacteristically serious tone asked, "Did something happen with you two?"

"No, not really... Not at all," she said with a shrug. "I just bumped into him yesterday and, I don't know. It was nothing, but it sort of felt like something."

"You're so far out of his league he was probably just shell-shocked at the sight of you, limo and all," Kay-Kay said with a giggle.

"Yeah, I'm being silly. Let's get back to it."

With that the girls resumed their work. Despite that she had decided to forget the nonsense with Jake, an hour later she again slowed down as she passed his apartment. The door stayed closed. When she got downstairs and opened the front door to leave the building surprise brushed across her face at the sight of him sitting on the hood of her car.

"Nice wheels. Much sexier than being driven around in that hearse, by that old corpse."

"Well I'm so glad you approve," she said sarcastically.

With that Jake jumped off the hood and walked right over to her. Face-to-face, barely inches apart, he asked, "Are you? Are you glad I approve?"

He smelled so good, and she thought about looking away but her gaze was locked onto his eyes. After a pause she said, "You're a player, obviously, and I need to go."

27

He smiled and looked down, which she now thought was a habit when he was called out, or at least when she called him out. Then he waved his hand in front of his body as if waving on royalty.

She shook her head and walked to her car door. Just before she put the key in the lock he said, "Come on. I waited for you, obviously. Let's go grab some pizza or something."

"I'm sorry, I'll be late. My parents will worry."

"Well then how about tomorrow? You can finish early with Kay-Kay so you won't even be late."

"I don't know."

"No big deal. I'll be home. If you happen to finish early and want to get some pizza knock on my door."

Paige smiled cautiously and got into her car. Jake stood watching as she pulled away. That night she could hardly fall asleep, consumed with memories of how he smelled.

The next day Paige nervously tapped her pencil on her notebook as Kay-Kay revised her outline for an upcoming school project. At one point Kay-Kay asked a question, and Paige accidently flicked her pencil, and it rolled off the bed. Not used to being clumsy she stumbled a bit as she bent over to pick it up. Half an hour later Paige nonchalantly said, "You seem like you're ready to start on the poster-board. I don't think you need me for that. Would you mind if I go and I'll see you tomorrow?"

"Sure, sounds good. Thanks for all of your help."

"I'm going to just use your bathroom before I go."

Paige looked herself over carefully as she lightly patted shimmery gloss on her lips. *Should I take my hair down?* she wondered. Her signature high ponytail wasn't her normal "date" hair. *Whatever it is, it isn't a date,* she told herself. Even more, she didn't want to give Jake the satisfaction that she had done anything special. Moments later she was at his door, knocking.

When he opened the door she instantly knew, whatever it was, it *was* something.

"Hey there. I knew you'd come."

"Well that's a shame. I do hate to be predictable," she quipped back.

He smiled and grabbed his leather jacket from the coatrack beside him. "Let's go."

As they walked away from the building, with a comfortable distance between them, Jake said, "My buddy works at a place a block from here. The pizza is good but the mozzarella sticks are the best you've ever had. You do eat, right? I know how girls like you are."

Paige flashed him the sarcastic smile she had mastered. "I eat."

Before a moment passed they had arrived at *Vinny's Pizza Parlor*. Jake held the door open for Paige, as he followed her into the neighborhood spot that smelled like Milan and New York swirled together, he was greeted with a chorus of, "Hey, Jake. Where you been, man?" from the guys working behind the counter.

"Ah, you know how it is," he said as he high-fived them over the counter.

"And your very beautiful friend?" one of the guys queried.

"Mikey, this is Paige. Paige, this is Mikey and the other boneheads," he said as he gestured towards them.

"It's nice to meet you," she said as she offered each a slight nod.

"Well, I can already tell you're too good for this guy," Mikey said with a laugh.

"Be nice," Jake said.

"Oh it's Ok, Jake. I already know it too," Paige said jokingly.

Jake's face turned red as he looked down, letting out a chuckle.

"Ah, she's got your number," another guy hollered.

"Ok, Ok. You've all had your fun. Paige why don't you grab us a table? Oh, what do you want to drink?"

"A diet Coke, please."

"Ah ha. Like I said, girls like you don't eat."

She shook her head and sat down. She heard Jake say, "A couple of slices and a large sticks," before he came to join her, bringing the sodas with him.

"Thank you."

"Food'll be ready in a few. So, how'd you meet Kay-Kay?"

Paige started telling him about the tutoring program and how she and Kay-Kay had bonded. When the food was ready Jake jumped up to get it. He pulled one of the mozzarella sticks apart to show her the hot, melted cheese. "But the sauce, it's the real Italian sauce that does it."

She dipped a stick into the marinara and took a bite. The hot cheese oozed in her mouth causing an explosion of tastes, and she wanted to remember them all. As she pulled the stick from her mouth a cheese string stuck to her lip. Jake smiled and then pointed to his own mouth and said, "You have a little something."

"Oh," she said before wiping it away.

"What did I tell you? Best sticks, right?"

"Yeah, they're great." All she could think about was the pull between her and Jake.

After that they continued eating and talking. When familiar subjects like Kay-Kay and school were exhausted they kept going, talking about their childhoods, families and hobbies. They talked long after the food was gone. Eventually, noticing it was getting dark out, Paige said, "I need to go soon."

"Ok, let's head out." But as soon as they left Jake said, "How about we take the long way back? I can give you a tour of the neighborhood."

"Sure."

They walked for nearly an hour, talking the whole time. Jake lived with his father who collected disability for a work-related injury. His mother had left them when he was little. Jake thought his father had abused her and "run her off." Paige also learned that Jake earned money by doing landscape work on the weekends. He planned to move into construction after graduation and had aspirations to run his own construction company but he didn't think it was realistic. He called it a pipedream. Jake wasn't anything like she expected. By the time they were back at her car they were holding hands, and she couldn't remember when that happened.

It was dark and they stood in the glow of the streetlight beside her car. As he looked into her eyes the only thing she was conscious of was that she was no longer conscious of anything. Her hand slipped from his as he leaned towards her, took her face gently into his hands, and kissed her. Moments later she was heading home. The next afternoon, and every school day afternoon to follow, she was with Jake.

*

At first she kept her relationship with Jake to herself. It wasn't that she wanted to keep it secret but rather it felt private and she didn't feel the need to share it. She also didn't know how to talk about it or who to tell. After a few weeks passed, she told Kay-Kay, and before long all of her friends knew. Despite the many obvious differences between them, Paige's friends accepted Jake without hesitation, at least the girls did. The guys in Paige's world didn't get it at all and often made comments. Sometimes when she walked down the hallway guys came up beside her and said, "So, you done slumming it? You ready for a real guy?" Paige didn't pay attention to any of it. She was well aware that those guys would do anything to be with her, and this was their pathetic way of trying to get her attention and showing each other they were "real guys." While her friends were secretly jealous, Paige was above it.

Paige and Jake never discussed their relationship either. They never said what they were to each other or that they were exclusive. They didn't need to. And despite Jake's history, Paige knew there was no one else. She felt completely secure in the extraordinary ordinariness of it all. She didn't think ahead.

The only people in Paige's life who didn't know about Jake were her parents. She hadn't done anything to draw attention to the changes in her life. She still got up early each morning to run, excelled in school and was engaged in numerous extracurricular activities. It wasn't that it was her intention to hide Jake from them. She allowed it to happen by spending time with him at school, his place and his neighborhood. They watched movies and television (usually comedies), listened to music (he was a heavy metal fan with posters of long-haired rockers plastered all over the walls of his sparse bedroom), kissed for hours on end, and they talked. They often took long walks all over Boston, talking about their lives and their dreams. Although Jake routinely talked about his aspirations, it was always tempered with self-doubt. He had never known anyone with "big dreams" who had achieved them. Paige used every chance she could to plant the seeds of hope in him. She said things like, "All things are possible if you believe in yourself and you're willing to work, which you are. I believe in you. You should go for it, don't hold back. Make your own luck." She was the only person in his life to ever say things like that to him, and when she said something was possible it actually felt possible. All she did to encourage him was returned to her tenfold. For example, Paige told him that she was thinking about studying art history someday. When he asked why she didn't just do art herself she told him about the pottery classes she had wanted to take that her mother disapproved of.

"You rich people, you're really something. All of that money and you don't even do the things you want to do."

"Hey, that's not fair," she said. But then he looked right through her and said, "You should do what you really want to do. I don't know much, but I know that."

"My mother is just, she's just very…"

"It's your life, isn't it?" he said, giving her hand a squeeze.

They got to each other, in every way, even when no one else did. It was effortless.

Soon the end of the school year was in sight. Jake, a year older than Paige, was graduating. He had lined up a job with a local construction company and planned to stick with his landscape work on weekends. He was going to continue living with his father until he could afford his own place which suited Paige since she used Kay-Kay as a cover when she wanted to stay at Jake's. He made no mention of it, but she thought that with her encouragement someday Jake would go to a community college to take some business classes and make his dream a reality.

Thanks to her own hard work and Paige's help, Kay-Kay found out that not only did she place out of her classes but she would be enrolled in honors classes for her sophomore year. Her mother invited Paige over for dinner to celebrate. Paige had grown very fond of Ms. Washington who treated her like a member of their extended family. She always enjoyed dinner at Kay-Kay's. Ms. Washington gave everyone a job to do to help get dinner ready and on the table, and then after a wonderful meal and spirited conversation, they all helped clean up. In a life structured around individual activities, Paige appreciated feeling like she was a part of a team. Sleepovers were her favorite. Trey would stay on the couch so the girls could be together. Paige loved flipping through Kay-Kay's latest fashion designs. She drew the most incredible outfits in the boldest colors. They would joke that someday Kay-Kay could make a gown for Eleanor.

Kay-Kay visited Paige's house many times too. Paige never warned people about her home, because there was no right way to do it. So the first time Kay-Kay came over, her jaw dropped as they drove up the winding private drive. "Shit girl, you have your own street?" Although the awe-factor never wore off, Kay-Kay was comfortable there, and they had many sleepovers, staying up all night and giggling. Kay-Kay routinely prodded Paige about her relationship with Jake, and although unprompted she always made sure to tell Paige that, "I haven't seen any other girls hanging around his place since he met you." Paige's parents invited Kay-Kay to several events at their home too, the kinds of silver-tray parties Kay-Kay, like most people, always wondered about. Paige's father took to Kay-Kay; she was forthright, witty, hard-working and loyal, all of the qualities he admired.

With the end of the school year summer vacation was around the corner. Normally, this meant months split between their beach homes. Paige couldn't bear the thought of being away from Jake all summer, so she convinced her parents to let her stay in town with Aggie so that she could take some college prep courses and continue tutoring Kay-Kay. Her parents reluctantly agreed but insisted that she come to Cape Cod for a couple of weeks at the end of the summer.

The next eight weeks were the best of her life. While people usually don't appreciate the great moments of life while they are happening, Paige did. Just like they had since the day they met, Paige and Jake each did their own thing and when they had free time, they spent it together. Paige signed up for two college prep courses at Wellesley College. Her days were spent running, swimming, taking classes and seeing Kay-Kay, as most of her other friends were away for the summer. Jake was at work during the days but they saw each other every night. When he was especially tired from work they would just lie in his bed and watch television. Other nights they went to a local bar, *Milligans*, which had a dance floor and deejay. His friend was a bouncer and stamped their hands even though they were underage. Jake usually had a couple of beers but Paige just drank water. All of Jake's buddies hung out there, drinking at the bar or shooting pool in the back room. Paige became friendly with the other guys' girlfriends as well as some regulars. When her own friends were in town they would come with them too. She always spent most of the night on the dance floor with the girls but she and Jake stared at each other, even if across the room from one another. He never stopped watching her for a minute and the sight of her having fun or doing a satirical sexy dance brought a little smile to his face. Whenever a Journey song like *Don't Stop Believin'* came on they sang on top of their lungs. When Journey's *Separate Ways* played they came together and held each other. The lyrics resonated with them both. It was their music. And no matter what, they always came together for the last song.

Most nights they walked slowly back to his place, holding hands, and talking. Then she drove home. As long as she came home at some point, Aggie let her be.

When Jake had a day off they went up to a small lake he knew about. There was a rope hanging from a tree they swung on, leaping into the cold water. Paige brought picnic lunches, and Jake brought a small Boom Box. By the end of July, Paige was ready and one night after a day at the lake they went back to Jake's and made love. She thought it was remarkable that someone as strong as Jake could be so gentle. Later that night, as they were falling asleep, he whispered, "You know I love you." She replied, "Yes, I know."

She hated leaving Jake to go to the Cape but she missed her father and was happy to get a chance to go to the beach. When she returned Kay-Kay was happy to tell her that while she was gone Jake worked extra hours and hung out alone at his place.

Paige's senior year flew by. Naturally she was accepted into all of the universities she applied to. Her top choices were Columbia and Harvard. She long imagined moving to New York for college and later to London for graduate school, but she wanted to be with Jake so she decided to go to Harvard. Her mother wanted her to go to Wellesley, like she had, but Paige was adamant about carving her own path. She never understood why her mother had spent so much time and energy on a college education just to spend her life hosting and attending parties. She once asked her mother if she had ever intended to do anything with her degree. Eleanor, never one to let anything slip by, replied, "Having interesting things to say to people is its own end. I hope you remember that." Paige didn't respond.

One afternoon at Jake's she casually told him that she planned to go to Harvard.

"Don't do that for me. You shouldn't change your life for me."

Taken aback she asked, "What do you mean?"

"I just don't want to be responsible for you staying here. You said you wanted to go to New York. Don't change things for me."

"Well, that's what people do, isn't it? And it's not like I'm staying here to go to some crummy school. I'd be at Harvard."

"Yeah, and you'd be under your mother's thumb, in a city you're bored of. And I'd be working all the time. I think you'd get sick of it."

Paige had no idea what was happening and where this was coming from. "Do you want me to leave? Is that what you're saying?"

"It's not that. I just know how things are, more than you, and I don't think you should make life choices you can't take back to hang here in this dump with me."

"I don't understand where this is coming from. Why are you saying this?"

"Shit, Paige. Let's not pretend we're in La La Land. Look around," he said loudly, flailing his arms widely. "I can't believe you're not sick of this yet, but you will be, you will be."

"I don't care about any of that," she said softly.

"Of course you don't care, you're loaded. You don't need to care. But I care. I fucking care."

He sat down on the edge of the bed while she just stood there. He had never spoken to her that way before.

"I didn't think any of that was an issue."

"Bullshit. Why haven't you ever brought me to your place, to meet your parents? Why do we always hang out here? Do you think I'm stupid? You care. You may not want to, but you fucking care."

She sat down next to him, and touched his face. "Look at me. Please, don't look down, look at me," she said softly. "I'm sorry. I should have introduced you to my family a long time ago. I honestly didn't think you wanted to meet them and…"

He cut her off, "It's Ok. I don't blame you."

"It's not like that, you're wrong. Please, let's just forget this craziness. I'm going to Harvard and I'm going to introduce you to my family."

"Paige, it's Ok."

"That's it. My mind is made up. Are you going to give me a hard time?" she asked in a teasingly way. He smiled a bit and then she coyly said, "Now, what should we do?" He grabbed her face, laughed, kissed her and then they tumbled down onto the bed and made love.

Later, while they were lying in bed and she rubbed the tips of his fingers he said, "I have to tell you something."

She looked up and smiled.

"I have a kid. His name is Casey. He's two."

Paige sat up, pulling the sheet up to cover herself. She shimmied backwards and folded her legs up. "What, what are you talking about?"

"I wanted to tell you, but…"

"But what? Two, did you say he's two? So the whole time we've been together, the whole time, you've been lying to me?"

"It isn't like that. I mean, it is, but I didn't mean it that way. His mother is just a girl I slept with a few times and she showed up on my doorstep like eight months pregnant, right before she was going to pop. I didn't even think the kid was mine. Then he was born and he had my eyes and I knew."

Paige sat perfectly still.

"It was just before I met you. I never cheated on you."

"You never cheated on me? You've been lying to me since the day we met! Do you see him? Do you see your son?"

"Yeah I see him. I go on weekends whenever I can."

Paige got up and started getting dressed.

"I made a mistake, Paige. I don't mean Casey is a mistake, I mean how can I say that, but I mean, I made a horrible mistake, but it was before I met you. I didn't tell you in the beginning and then I didn't know how to tell you. I didn't want to fuck everything up. I just wanted to keep you separate from all that. You have nothing to do with who I was then."

Paige sat on the edge of the bed to zip up her shoes. He touched her shoulder and she pulled away.

"This is why I didn't tell you. I knew this would happen."

Paige stood up and turned to face him. "You didn't tell me because you're a coward. I mean, my god, you have a child, a child and you didn't tell me. All those weekends you said you were working. You lied to me over and over again. I have to go. I don't know who you are or anything. We're done. There's nothing more to say."

Paige left and got into her car. Knowing he might be looking out of his window watching her she sped away and then pulled over two blocks away. She sat and cried and cried. *What just happened?* played over and over again in her mind.

She called Kay-Kay that night and as soon as she said hello, Paige asked, "Did you know? Did you know he has a child?"

"Oh shit, Paige."

"Did you know?"

"I heard rumors but I never asked him and he never told me. I didn't know for sure. I'm so sorry, Paige."

"I gotta go," Paige said as she hung up the phone.

She enrolled in Columbia the next day and moved to New York that August.

*

Paige spent her first few months at Columbia focused entirely on her studies. Her father had secured her a private suite in the dorms so she had plenty of time alone. Despite everyone's friendliness, she mostly kept to herself. She stuck to a strict routine of running, classes and studying. In her free time she visited art museums and went to movies. She missed Kay-Kay and thought about Jake endlessly. When she returned home for Thanksgiving break there were two messages on her answering machine from Kay-Kay. The first said: "Paige, I'm so sorry I didn't give you a head's up but I didn't know for sure. Call me. I'm worried about you." The next message, left a week later said: "I heard you're in New York now, please call me if you get this. I miss you. I don't know if you care but I hardly ever see Jake anymore. No one sees him much. He just goes to work and he's like a hermit at home. We don't have to talk about him if you don't want, just call me and let me know if you're Ok." Paige thought about calling her back but she didn't.

She returned to school and resumed her routine but she couldn't stop thinking about Jake. As time passed, she started to feel sorry for him, and she regretted how things ended. She also felt terrible for cutting Kay-Kay off. Paige felt lonely without her. She realized her anger had been displaced. She hoped to reconnect with Kay-Kay over Christmas break and possibly see Jake and give him a chance to explain.

The day after Christmas she picked up the phone, took a deep breath and called Kay-Kay.

"Hello."

"Kay-Kay? It's me, Paige."

"Whoa... God, Paige. I never thought I'd hear from you again."

"Yeah, I know… Kay-Kay I'm so sorry I just left for school with no word and that I never returned your calls. It's no excuse but I was just going through a really hard time."

"It's Ok, I get it," Kay-Kay said, still sounding caught off guard by Paige's call.

"So, how are you? How's school?" Paige asked.

"Uh, it's fine. I had to take the SATs which were awful but mostly it's fine. I like being in the good classes but it's a lot of work."

"And Jake? How's Jake?"

Kay-Kay made a sound as if she was about to answer when Paige said, "I was thinking of seeing him. I miss him."

In a lowered voice Kay-Kay responded, "Oh shit Paige, I need to tell you something."

"What is it Kay-Kay?"

"I'm afraid telling you know will screw things up but if I don't tell you, I'm, as bad as Jake and why you got so mad at him, and then…" Kay-Kay trailed off as she tried to work through her thoughts.

Paige interrupted with, "Kay-Kay, just tell me what's going on."

Kay-Kay was silent and Paige took a breath before asking, "Has he moved on? Is he with someone?"

"It's not that, well not really." There was a long pause before Kay-Kay continued, "Something happened… with me and Jake. It was after Thanksgiving and we were both depressed and hanging out and it, it just happened but it was just a mistake and I'm afraid you'll hear it from him if you call him so… I know you hate me right now but please don't because it was just a dumbass thing and I really miss you."

Paige quietly responded, "I don't hate you. Thank you for telling me," and then she hung up.

She grabbed a decorative pillow from her bed, held it as tightly as she could, hunched over and rocked back and forth. Then she started crying, and she couldn't stop. *How could they?* played over and over in her mind. Afraid Kay-Kay would call back, she unplugged the phone and then fell over on the stack of pillows on her bed. Eventually she fell asleep.

When she woke up hours later there were two messages on her answering machine, both were from Jake. In the first he said: "Hey… it's me. I don't know what to say. I don't know why Kay-Kay told you that, it was just a stupid thing. I feel like I should say sorry but we weren't together and I hadn't heard from you and… I don't know what else to say." In the second message he said: "Hey, listen… I don't want to bother you if you don't want to hear from me so I won't call again but I miss you and I'm sorry. I love you. Always will."

She spent the rest of her school break crying and vowed never to let anyone betray her again. She returned to Columbia in January.

*

With a double major in art history and international studies Paige had plenty of schoolwork to fill her time. She discovered women's studies in her second semester and felt as if she found a missing puzzle piece. The writings of great feminist scholars gave her a language to understand her experiences and to speak about the inequalities that had always troubled her. Through her new exposure to feminist authors she even came privately, to, forgive Jake. He had been shaped by forces he couldn't see and he was using what he had to push back, to feel worthy. It wasn't as easy for her to resolve her feelings about Kay-Kay. Just as soon as she would start to forgive, thinking Jake, a player, had clearly taken advantage of her, she felt guilty for not allowing Kay-Kay the dignity of owning her choices. It was a conundrum she couldn't reconcile. From then on she took as many women's studies courses as she could fit into her already busy schedule. She was desperate for answers.

She easily made friends, although she instinctively kept a comfortable distance between her and them. She was as disciplined with her emotions as with her daily exercise regime and learned never to reveal herself. She also never lacked for male attention.

Occasionally she dated although she found most guys predictable and boring. The guys in her social circle reeked of the entitlement and accompanying arrogance she loathed. It wasn't until her junior year that she met someone special, in the most unexpected way.

While home for Thanksgiving her mother insisted that she seek out the son of one of her father's business associates when she returned to school. Their family name was Bradley, and Eleanor was all-too happy to espouse their virtues. Although she had never met the son in question Eleanor insisted, "He comes from good stock and it would be rude if you didn't reach out to him since you attend the same university."

"Oh mother, I beg you to let this go," Paige pleaded.

"I will give Mrs. Bradley your contact information so the young man can call you," Eleanor responded.

Paige continued to implore her not to but it was impossible to gauge if Eleanor intended to comply.

Several weeks later Paige found herself at a small holiday party at an off-campus apartment. It wasn't the typical student's apartment but rather a palatial bachelor pad in a full-service building with a doorman. Paige was invited by a friend of a friend.

She was sitting with a small group of friends when a guy she had never seen before came over and started introducing himself to the group. His name was Spencer. Although she was not one for clichés Paige instantly thought the only way to describe him was dashing. He was tall with dirty blonde hair that fell in perfect wisps towards one of his brown eyes. Dressed in jeans, a white polo shirt and an exquisite dark brown blazer that matched his eyes and accentuated his broad shoulders, he was movie-star gorgeous. She had never seen a guy that looked so effortlessly together. When he shook Paige's hand he held on for a moment and smiled warmly. Before long the two of them were engrossed in their own private conversation. Ten minutes into their conversation one of the girls standing nearby, and not so subtly trying to work her way into the conversation, alluded to Spencer's family money with a comment about being "set for life." Before Spencer could respond Paige looked at the interloper and said, "I think people should make their

41

own way in this world, especially when they have the means to do so."

Spencer smiled and returned his full attention to Paige, saying, "I couldn't agree more. And so many, the majority in fact, don't have that privilege. I mean look what happens to kids born into extreme poverty. I think about the famines in so much of the world and wonder why we let it persist. And then you look at girls and how girls are denied even basic education in much of the world and it just makes you want to do something, right?"

"Uh, yeah, it does," Paige said, shocked to meet someone aware of the things she cared about so deeply. After that they spoke for nearly two hours before Paige said, "Well, it's pretty late and it looks like my friends are ready to go. Do you want to head back to campus with us?"

"I would love to but I can't. I have to clean up. This is my apartment."

Paige giggled. She was surprised and a bit embarrassed. "Oh, I didn't realize. I came with some friends."

"I know. I asked them to invite you."

Paige looked perplexed.

"I should have said something sooner but we were so involved in our conversation. You see my stepmother told me I absolutely had to meet you. I dreaded the idea of a fix-up by my stepmother, but since she was so insistent I thought I'd host a little get together. Had I known how incredible you were, I wouldn't have invited all of these people."

"Who is your stepmother?" Paige asked, irritated.

"Liza Bradley. I'm sorry. I don't think we did last names. I'm Spencer Bradley."

Paige stood up abruptly and said, "Spencer, I don't like games and I certainly don't like being a pawn in yours. Good night."

He jumped up and gently touched her arm as she turned to walk away. "Please, forgive me. It isn't like that at all. If you knew my stepmother and her friends you'd understand. I assumed she'd set me up with some mindless princess interested in the Bradley name and money, as she was. I'm pretty sure that was her motivation for marrying my dad. The get together was a way to get her off my back. She's relentless and I didn't want to meet another girl in school to get her M.R.S."

Paige stared at him in silence.

"Please, you're amazing and I'm mortified. Please tell me I haven't ruined something that just began."

Paige gave him a stern look. He seemed entirely sincere. "I respect people who are forthright," she said.

"Understood. I do too and if you're willing to give me a chance I will forever be an open book."

She smiled slightly.

"So does this mean I can see you again Paige Michaels?"

She hesitated for a moment and smirked before saying. "Yes, I'll see you again Spencer Bradley, despite our families."

From that point on they were an item. Eleanor and Liza were thrilled but Paige and Spencer didn't let that spoil their fun.

*

Paige and Spencer used their relationship as a means of figuring out who they were as individuals and simultaneously they built themselves an identity as a couple. They attended college-wide lectures, participated in activist groups, spent Spring Break on a humanitarian trip to El Salvador and spent the first semester of their senior year abroad doing internships in London. They stayed part of an elite social group although, by their own choice, they were as much on the outside as on the inside. There were several times when someone on the peripheries of their set would make a play for one of them, but neither was tempted nor were either needlessly jealous. They were entirely secure with themselves and each other.

After graduation Spencer pursued his MBA while Paige did a rigorous internship for WIN, an international women's rights organization. They were married the summer Spencer graduated in what was the social event of the year. Knowing their mothers would be relentless they took the path of least resistance and simply let Eleanor and Liza plan the over-the-top event for more than five hundred people Paige and Spencer didn't know or care about. They were able to just focus on each other during it all. Although they never said it out loud, they also thought it was one of the last hoops they would have to jump through.

They welcomed their daughter Chloe into the family the following summer. Paige was in love with Chloe from the start. More than anything, Chloe brought laughter into Paige's daily life—whether it was splashing water in the bathtub, a tickle-fest on the couch, or telling silly bedtime stories—Paige never missed a chance to smile and giggle with her daughter.

Soon, following in his father's footsteps, Spencer was one of the most respected and feared real estate developers in New York. Never one to lose track of his ethical compass, or deny Paige's wishes, he made time for charitable projects including footing the bill for several community gardens throughout New York's boroughs. Paige assumed a leadership position for the women's rights organization she came to see as 'where she was meant to serve.' Her work centered on fundraising efforts—which her colleagues understood she was uniquely positioned for. She made a point of travelling annually to impoverished nations to be with some of the world's most exploited women and children whom she worked to help. Despite the demands of her work she always made time to actively participate in Chloe's upbringing and the two were very close. In order to be available to Chloe, Paige moved out of the WIN offices to work primarily from her lavish home office. In what was otherwise a pristine office suit decorated with white furniture, draperies and parquet floors, there was one area reserved for Chloe. Over the years that space alone changed, from a playpen filled with toys to a small table and chairs for tea parties and eventually an ivory Victorian fainting couch where Chloe could lay down and tell Paige about her day. Her life was a mix of motherhood, service work (which over time came to mostly involve planning fundraising galas and "awareness" events) and making appearances at social events for Spencer's business. Paige knew how to appear bright and shiny in public and moved seamlessly between her roles. Time moved on, and without catastrophe or even incident, Paige's life appeared to be charmed to all those watching.

CHAPTER 4

When Eleanor Michaels was diagnosed with breast cancer she took the news with the same stoic dignity that characterized her life. With a bleak prognosis she refused the standard of care and decided to live the remainder of her life quietly in one of the family's vacation homes. She loved the autumn on Cape Cod and was glad to take advantage.

Paige met her parents at the vacation house shortly after they settled in. For three days she woke up at the crack of dawn, went running, showered and was sitting in the sunlit breakfast room with a fresh pot of coffee made by the time Eleanor came downstairs. She fixed her mother's breakfast after which they sat on the front porch, looking out at the beach and flipping through magazines. They went into town each day and popped around the shops or just had lunch at their favorite Inn. On the fourth morning Eleanor sat down at the table and Paige handed her a coffee cup and said, "Your eggs will be ready in a moment."

Eleanor shook her head. "That can wait. Come sit," she said as she waved her over. Paige sat down next to her mother and looked earnestly at her.

Eleanor smiled slightly and Paige followed suit. "Listen dear, this has been lovely but now it's time for you to get back to your life."

Paige was surprised and quickly responded, "Mother, this is exactly where I need to be."

Eleanor shook her head and said, "Nonsense. Things must carry on. You have responsibilities you must attend to. You shouldn't be here, boiling eggs for me."

"But mother, I'm happy to be here."

"Well that's lovely, but not very practical. You must carry on with business as usual. We all must. Remember, always stay on course." Eleanor placed her hand on Paige's, squeezed it lightly, smiled and said, "Now that's settled, go back to your life."

Before Paige could respond Eleanor stood up and started walking away.

"But mother, what about your breakfast?"

"Leave the eggs to Aggie, you've been overcooking them and I haven't wanted to hurt your feelings," she said as she left the room.

Paige packed her things, and hugged her parents tightly, whispering "I love you" to them each, before returning to New York.

Eleanor died, without pain, less than two months later.

Surprisingly, Spencer seemed to be hit the hardest by Eleanor's premature passing. Paige knew it brought up memories of the terrible loss of his own mother. After catching his father with another woman, his mother had committed suicide when he was ten years old. Elise Bradley sat in her car in the garage with the engine running. Spencer had gone to a friend's house after school that day and thus was home later than usual. He always wondered if she had really intended to kill herself or if it was just a cry for attention. He lived with enormous guilt and never fully came to terms with it. Unlike Paige's detached relationship with Eleanor, Spencer had been extremely close with his mother. He had wonderful memories of his mother building magical tents in his room under which they read stories and talked about their dreams. She had been quite the dreamer. He had long-ago tried to brush these memories aside but Eleanor's death brought it all back and he became distant.

Paige oversaw the planning of her mother's funeral. Eleanor had requested a small service for immediate family only. To Paige's surprise her note read, "I spent my life in the world of social events. I think I shall spend my hereafter more privately." Determined to honor her wishes, Paige made certain every detail would have met with Eleanor's approval. The casket was surrounded by flawless white tea roses. Paige thought her mother would have been pleased. Paige wondered what her father would do with Eleanor gone so soon. Although her parents were, to many, the paradigmatic American couple, Paige never knew if that was merely a role they played. At the reception after the funeral she overheard her cousins talking about John. One said, "He'll have women all over him. I bet he'll be remarried by next year." Paige thought that was ridiculous and that he would at minimum take the requisite year to grieve. If he did eventually seek a companion she never doubted it would be a woman of good standing. What she never could have anticipated is that merely sixteen months after her mother passed her father would be gone.

*

Paige, Spencer and Chloe arrived in Wellesley the day before the funeral. They were greeted by Aggie who hugged Paige tightly while weeping. "Who would have guessed a man as fit as your father would have a heart attack?" she asked through her tears. "I can't believe he's gone." Numb and exhausted, Paige let Aggie embrace her although she couldn't manage to hug her in return.

"Aggie, can you have our things taken to the guest rooms please?" Paige said in a monotone. Aggie signaled to the other staff members who nodded their heads at Paige as a sign of respect for her father before leading the family to their rooms. Halfway there Paige said, "There's no need to accompany us, thank you Aggie."

Before walking away Aggie gently took Paige's hand. Paige turned and looked at her and Aggie said, "I'm just so sorry, Paige. I know how much you loved him. Please let me know how I can help you."

"Thank you, Aggie," Paige said in a trance. She pointed Chloe to a room down the hall, and she and Spencer went into their room. Paige immediately walked over to the luggage that had been laid out on a bench and started unpacking. Spencer walked up behind her, squeezed her arms and said, "Let the staff do that." She turned and looked at him without saying a word. "This is terrible, I know, what can I do?" he asked.

"Nothing. I'm fine. I just want to get past tomorrow," she said before resuming her unpacking.

"I still don't like the idea of leaving you here," he said. "I can take off as much time as we need."

"I'll be fine. Aggie and the others are here and I don't know how long it will take me to sort through their things and deal with the estate. Chloe can't miss school so early into the semester and I don't want to send her home alone."

"She'll be fine with Gert. At least let me stay to help you deal with the lawyers."

Paige continued to focus on her unpacking. "I'll be fine. Chloe lost two of her grandparents and she's under enormous pressure in school right now. One of us should be there with her and there's nothing you can do here that Aggie and the others can't help with. Honestly, it would be easier to go through it all with them, they know where everything is."

Spencer didn't say anything for a moment and then said, "You may feel differently tomorrow. If you do, just say the word. For that matter, after I take Chloe home and get her settled I can come back at any time."

"I'll be fine," she said, while refolding a white shirt. "I think I should go downstairs and chat with Aggie about the arrangements for tomorrow, to make sure all the out-of-towners are taken care of and that there isn't anything she needs from me. Will you finish the unpacking?"

Spencer nodded.

The next morning Paige opened her eyes when she heard Spencer getting dressed. "What time is it?" she asked sleepily.

"It's 7:30. I'm sorry if I woke you. Did you get any sleep?"

"A bit. My nerves were stronger than that sleeping pill though. I just want to get through this day," she said as she sat up and stretched her arms.

"The driver is picking us up at 9:00 so we can get there before everyone arrives. Shall I have Aggie send up breakfast?"

"Just some coffee," she responded as she stood up and made her way to the bathroom.

"I'll have Aggie send up some fruit and a soft boiled egg in case you want to nibble. It may be hard for you to eat later with everyone here."

Paige waved her hand up as a sign she heard him before stepping into the shower.

Four hours later the service was ending. Unlike her mother's funeral, Paige played no role in orchestrating the massive remembrance to her father. Politicians and a splattering of Forbes wealthiest had jetted in from all over. Although they were unable to attend, the President and First Lady sent a handwritten note with their condolences. Paige was particularly glad to see the many true friends John had amassed over his extraordinary life. She was especially touched to see his childhood friends there, most of whom led modest lives that bore little resemblance to her father's adult life. Seeing the deep sense of loss on their faces made her think about what a good, loyal and loved man her father was. As the service ended Spencer walked Paige and Chloe up the aisle. Paige made sure to look at as many people as she could. She made a conscious effort to exhibit her appreciation for the remarkable sea of people who had come. It wasn't until she was almost at the end that she saw a face that made her gasp: Jake. He looked older, and a bit worse for wear, but his piercing blue eyes were as magnetic as they had always been. She turned her head slowly towards him, and he nodded discreetly. Before she knew it, she was in the car heading back to her family home for the reception. Spencer and Chloe were talking but it just sounded like white noise. All she could think about was Jake.

For the next several hours she managed to make small talk with everyone who approached her. It was difficult to take in all of the stories about how her father had given someone their first break or done them some favor, but ever-appropriate she allowed each person the opportunity to share their memories. Throughout the day she casually darted her eyes around the room to see if Jake was there. He wasn't. After the guests left and the staff began cleaning up Paige insisted that Spencer and Chloe head back to New York. Both Spencer and Chloe tried to protest but at Paige's insistence that they "not let their lives fall apart" they eventually acquiesced and left. Before walking out the door Spencer hugged Paige and said, "If you want me to come back I can be here within a couple of hours." Paige reminded him to make sure Chloe remembered to attend the Columbia event and then gave him a quick kiss and sent them on their way.

*

That night she lay in bed remembering what it had been like living in her parents' house. It felt smaller than when she was a child, but it was only now that she understood its grandeur. She thought about Jake and how disconcerting yet strangely comforting it was seeing him. She considered looking him up to thank him for paying his respects, but she forced herself to push these thoughts aside and focus on getting through the following day.

The next morning she skipped both her run and breakfast. She dressed in a simple black skirt suit and pearls to meet with the estate lawyer. As expected, her parents left everything to her and Chloe, minus deserved allotments for long-time staff members as well as generous charitable donations. Paige was profoundly moved to learn her parents had left a multi-million dollar donation to WIN. She intended to prepare the Wellesley estate for auction and hold onto the vacation homes for the time being.

She spent the next day walking through the large house identifying items that should be packed for charity and those to be distributed to family members as Aggie and the other staff members documented her wishes. She also encouraged the staff to take items for themselves. Never one for sentimentality, she didn't want anything for herself except for her father's favorite gold watch. When Paige was little and he was rushing out to fly to a meeting somewhere he always hugged her and then tapped his watch gently and said, "Time is ticking. Tick Tock" to which she replied, "Tick Tock," and the two shared a smile.

The next day she ran a mile further than usual before getting to the difficult task of going through her father's personal items. She sifted through letters, business documents and photo albums. Sitting on the floor of her father's mammoth private study as the sunlight peered through the draped windows, bringing lightness into the dark mahogany room she came across a weathered handwritten note:

"Ellie, you must know it isn't your fault. I'm so sorry this happened to you. I love you. Please be well. We can try again. John"

Paige put the note in her pocket and continued sorting through the piles before her. An hour later as she was having lunch with Aggie she pulled the note out of her pocket and slid it across the table. Aggie looked at it and Paige said, "I found this in my father's things. Do you know what it's about?"

Aggie gave Paige a serious look and Paige continued, "Try again? Does this mean my mother had a miscarriage? Did they want to have more children or was this before me?"

"Paige, sometimes the past is better left in the past. Children aren't meant to know everything about their parents."

"Aggie, I have always relied on you to be candid. My mother didn't exactly prioritize mothering, as you know better than anyone, so this strikes me as curious. If you know what it refers to, please tell me."

"You should prepare yourself."

"What is it Aggie?"

Aggie hesitated before continuing, "I didn't work for them at the time but I heard from others and a bit from your father when he first hired me. I think it was a couple of years before you were born. Your mother was pregnant and they were attending an event. I think right in town here. I don't know all of the details but your parents separated at the event and your mother was attacked. Paige, she was sexually assaulted and beaten by a man in a coat check room and later had a miscarriage. I heard she withdrew terribly after that but your father, your father brought her back. I was hired during your mother's last trimester with you. Your father told me it had been 'a difficult pregnancy' and that she was depressed. He asked me to let him know if she ever acted 'unusually' or in a way that was 'cause for concern' as he put it. He said to interrupt him no matter where he was or what he was doing. Of course your mother never said a word to me and once you were born we were all focused on you and there was never mention again."

Paige stood up and looked at Aggie. "Thank you. Thank you for telling me."

"Paige," Aggie called, to stop her from leaving.

"Yes, Aggie."

"Forgive me for saying it, but I know your mother may have been a bit, a bit distant in some ways."

Paige blinked to show she was listening.

"There are some things that happen to us, deep violations, and if we never heal ourselves, well, we're altered if we never heal."

Paige walked over and gave Aggie a kiss on the top of her head. "Thank you, sweet Aggie."

She then calmly walked out of the room. She stood in the foyer trying to decide if she should return to her father's office or go upstairs to bed. She did neither. She grabbed her handbag and coat from the stand beside the front door and left. After wandering around the property for a few minutes she took her cellphone out of her handbag and scrolled through her address book. There was no one listed she wanted to call. She dialed 411. An hour later she met Jake at a coffee shop.

*

When she arrived she saw Jake sitting at a small table right in the center of the coffee shop. Most people would pick a table off to the side or in a corner, but not him. Jake was unabashedly and unmistakably right there. It was comforting to know that could still be counted on, and she smiled ever so slightly as she approached him. He stood up but seemed unsure what to do, and so he awkwardly pulled a chair out for her. They sat down, and he smiled, revealing badly stained and damaged teeth she wished she hadn't seen. His once thick mane of hair was now tied in a straggly ponytail. He said "hey" softly and in hearing his voice Paige was instantly able to see past the signs of wear and tear to the Jake she remembered. He had physically aged more than she, but he was unchanged.

"Do you want something?" he asked nervously as he again stood up. Before she could respond he was slowly moving towards the counter.

"Coffee, black please," she said.

Moments later he returned with two mugs and placed one down before her.

"Thank you," she said, as she gently placed her hand on his.

He sat down and peered across the table intensely. Finally he softly asked, "How are you?"

She shrugged and said, "I honestly don't know."

"The service was a great tribute. I've never seen so many people at a funeral before. Your father must have been a great guy, like you always said."

She smiled. "I was surprised to see you there. I, I looked for you at the reception after but..."

"I saw the announcement in the Globe and I remembered how much you loved him. I wanted to pay my respects. I didn't think I should go to your house after, uh, I, uh..."

She squeezed her eyes shut in an extended blink, offered a closed-mouthed smile and shook her head as if to tell him the past was past. "I'm very touched you came. Means a lot. Thank you. And thank you for coming here now. I, I just..." but he cut her off.

"I was happy to come. Whatever you need. I'm here."

She tilted her head in acknowledgement. "So, why don't you tell me about you. What do you do?"

"Same old, same old. Mostly house painting and landscape work. Used to do construction too, and I had a pretty good gig but things have dried up so, you know."

"And your son, Casey, how is he?"

Jake looked taken aback. "Uh, he's good, he's good. I have a daughter now too actually, Marie, she's ten. Gonna be a real heartbreaker"

"And, their mother?" Paige asked.

"Different mothers, and they can't stand each other and you know, I do what I can to help each of them but we're not together. Been on my own for a while now, less hassles I guess."

Paige smiled.

"And you, what about your life?" he asked with great interest.

"I live in New York. I never left after college. And I work for WIN. It's an international women's network. We try to help exploited women and children all over the world, mostly those who have been trafficked and prostituted or raped due to conflict where they live and that kind of thing. Probably more than you want to know."

Jake's eyes opened widely. "Wow. Good for you. That's great, really great. So I guess you didn't do something in art. I always figured you might be an artist by now."

"I studied art history in school but I never," she trailed off as Jake asked, "And your family?"

"My husband, Spencer, is a real estate developer. We met in school. And Chloe, our daughter, she's getting ready to graduate high school and start college in September."

"She's beautiful, reminded me of you at that age, except her hair is lighter."

Paige blushed. "Well, she's certainly her own person. She thinks she's in love and she's making all kinds of plans."

"Maybe she is in love. Just because you're young doesn't mean your feelings aren't real."

There was a pause and Paige wanted to change the subject. "Have you ever been to New York? There's a lot to do. And great pizza places."

He shook his head and quietly said, "I've never been anywhere."

She felt a lump in her throat. "Well, it's never too late, right?"

He smiled a little, but she knew it was only to make her feel better.

There was a long silence and then Paige asked, "Do you know if Kay-Kay ever made it to New York, to the fashion institute?

Jake looked surprised. "Um, yeah, she did actually. From what I heard from Ms. Washington she only went to the school for a year though. I know she worked as a seamstress for a while and then had a little dress shop, in Brooklyn I think, but that was years ago so I'm not sure where she is these days. I really stopped hanging out with her soon after you left for college and... and we drifted. I used to help her mother with some things and she would tell me about

Kay-Kay though, but eventually she and Trey moved and then I did and..." he shrugged.

"Well, good for Kay-Kay that she made it to F.I.T. She was so determined. I always hoped she'd make it. I've often thought about her and..." she trailed off as Jake reached across the table and put his hand on hers.

"Paige, I'm so sorry I..." but she again hard blinked her eyes, smiled and shook her head. "We don't need to, it's Ok."

He nodded.

They just sat there, peaceful and silent, with his hand on hers. Eventually Jake said, "You know, you're skin and bones. You've always been a string bean but something tells me it has been a while since you've eaten just about anything. You want to go grab a bite in the old neighborhood?"

She smiled and nodded. It felt good to be taken care of by him. In fact it felt good to feel anything.

The next thing she knew they were at the old pizza place. She was struck that a couple of the once-young guys behind the counter were still there, but with changed faces. Soon the tastes of hot cheese and marinara were exploding in her mouth. It was the most comforting sensation as each bite warmed her from the inside out. Jake made sure she ate a "good meal," as he called it, and they talked. They talked about high school, their jobs and their families. Paige told Jake all about her father. She also told him about the note and what Aggie had told her about her mother. She said, "My mother always made me feel like she didn't support my work but now I am thinking..."

"Now you're thinking it was just too painful for her, too close to home."

"Yes, exactly," she said.

"Sometimes there are things we can't deal with because we're not strong enough so we need to push them out of our minds. I'm sure she was proud of you."

Soon they were walking around the old neighborhood as the sky darkened, talking about movies, music and other remarkably trivial things. "We're just a couple of blocks from *Milligans*. Should we go for a drink?"

"*Milligans* is still there?" Paige asked in disbelief.

"Yup, sure is. It's actually bigger. They took over the place next door and added some tables and they serve bar food now like wings and sliders. The crowd isn't the same as the old days but I still hang sometimes. Want to check it out?"

"Sure, let's go."

*

As Jake swung the door open, she was bombarded by the bright lights, noise and music. It was loud and crowded. He ushered her in with care, and then she watched as he high-fived the bouncer and then waved to the bartender. He led her to the one open bar stool where she sat down.

"What'll you have?" he asked.

"Oh, I guess I'll just have a white wine."

"Jimmy, whatever you got on tap and a white wine for my friend."

As Jimmy slid the drinks over he smiled at Paige and said, "Watch out for this one, a nice gal like you. You're too good for him."

"So I've been told," Paige replied, as she broke out into laughter.

Jake blushed and then said, "It's great to see you smile."

"Even at your expense?" she asked sarcastically.

"Especially then."

Time flew as they joked with each other, chatted with people at the bar and even playfully teased Jimmy as he was slammed with "foo-foo" drink orders from some local college kids. After a couple of drinks Paige said, "The music isn't like I remember. It sucks, doesn't it? What happened to the deejay?"

"They got rid of him ages ago the cheap bastards. There's a jukebox now but the college crew come in and load it up with whiny guitar top-40 crap or even worse, radio hip-hop. You've gotta drink just to tune it out." Then, signaling to the bartender he hollered, "Jimmy, can you get me some quarters?" as he slid a couple of bucks across the bar. "Wait right here," he said as he took his change and headed to the jukebox.

When he returned he said, "Now we have a few more songs to get through so be patient."

She smiled. Before long, *Don't Stop Believin'* came on and the entire place exploded into cheers. Everyone was singing along. She suddenly felt transported. As the greatest hits of their high school days played on they jumped on the dance floor and started singing, dancing and laughing. When she heard the opening beats of *Separate Ways* she shut her eyes and leaned into him. She felt bodies jumping around them as they swayed ever-so-slowly, just holding each other. And then, as the chorus swelled, he started whispering along in her ears.

An hour later they were in his apartment making love.

*

The next morning Paige woke up at the first sunlight with a singular thought: *What have I done?* She slithered out of bed and started putting her clothes on. As she was buttoning up her blouse Jake opened his eyes. "What are you doing?" he asked groggily.

"I have to go," she said, quickening the pace with which she dressed.

"Whoa, hold on," he said as he sat up and put his hand out.

"I can't, I have to go," she said as she slipped her shoes on.

"So that's it? You're just going to leave?" he asked.

She stopped, looked at him and said, "I've made a terrible mistake, and I need to go."

"Paige, don't say that. Last night was, it was amazing. Please don't run off, we can figure this out."

"Figure this out? There's nothing to figure out Jake, I have a family. I'm married and last night..." she searched for words as he interjected, "Last night wasn't nothing. It wasn't just a mistake and you know it."

59

"Jake, I, I wasn't thinking clearly. I was so sad about my father and I just learned this awful thing happened to my mother and I wasn't myself."

"I think you were more yourself than you normally let yourself be, and that's what scares you."

"Jake, you should have known I wasn't thinking clearly, but you didn't care. You weren't thinking about me at all."

"Hey, you called me," he snapped back. Then he took a breath and more calmly said, "You called me. Don't you think it was for a reason?"

"I needed a friend, but you're right, I called you. I called you and I shouldn't have and I have to live with that."

She turned to leave and he said, "So that's it? You're really just going to leave? Why do you always run away from the people you love?"

She turned to face him and said, "I will always have a very special place in my heart for you, but the people I am committed to are my husband and my daughter, despite my carelessness."

"You didn't say love. You didn't say you love him. Maybe you married the wrong guy. When did you meet him, right after me? Maybe it was a mistake. You didn't just end up with someone, you came to me."

"Jake, there's no point to this. I'm married. No matter what is said, it ends with me leaving."

"Of course it does. That's what you do."

"That's not true."

"Isn't it? What about Kay-Kay? Why did you abandon her?"

"That's not what happened and you know it."

"It isn't? When you found out about Casey and ran off to New York you never called her, never saw her, cut her off completely. She didn't understand why. She thought you didn't care about her. Tell me, what had Kay-Kay done to you?"

Paige took a deep breath and sat down on the corner of the bed. "I let Kay-Kay go because in my mind I couldn't separate her from you. When I thought of her I thought of you and so I let the friendship go. And you're right, it wasn't fair to her at all. I had hoped to reconnect with her but then I heard about the two of you and, and well, that was it, there was no way back."

He leaned closer to her and softly said, "Paige, I'm so sorry for what happened with Kay-Kay. I've carried it with me all of these years. It's my biggest regret. We had both been missing you, and she was so hurt, and, and we just wanted to feel better. It was stupid and I hated myself for it."

"Jake, what do you want me to say? This was so long ago and I've let it go and you should too."

"Paige, you were the best thing that's ever happened to me and I blew it. I would give anything to go back."

"Jake, it was probably over with us long before Kay-Kay. The fact is, even if you forget the ugly bits, we were so young."

"What was I to you, a community service project like Kay-Kay?"

Paige pulled back and stood up. "My friendship with Kay-Kay was very real and completely genuine and so were my feelings for you. I was in love with you."

"You sure you weren't just seeing how the other half lived, like an afterschool activity? You just needed an excuse to leave and I gave you one."

"Jake, I'm truly sorry if you think that, but that's on you, not me. I know the loss I felt was real." She picked up her handbag and walked to the door.

"Wait, Paige I love you. I love you," he said longingly.

"Jake, you have an idea of me, an idea from a long time ago and I guess I had one of you too. If you loved me you would want my life to be better, not worse. I know you mean it or at least you think you do, but whether or not you had feelings for me never really was the problem, was it?" She paused before continuing, "You should have told me about your son. You kept the most important thing in your life from me."

"You wouldn't have understood," he said.

"If you would have seen in you what I saw in you, maybe you would have trusted it all more. But you're right, we'll never really know. It doesn't matter, the time is gone. Goodbye, Jake. I wish all good things for you. I truly do."

With that, Paige opened the apartment door and left. Despite what she had told Jake, images of him looking into her eyes, touching her and kissing her flashed in her mind like a strobe light. And even if she could suppress the flashes, something he said had seeped in. She wandered the neighborhood looking for a cab, with one question playing over and over again in her mind: *Did I marry the wrong man?*

*

For the next two days, Paige busied herself with the tasks associated with getting her parents' estate in order in an effort to try and forget what she had done, but her conscience was heavy with guilt when she returned to New York. Spencer was waiting as she walked off of their plane. He put his arm around her, asked their driver to put her bags in the car, and whisked her home. As they passed by the doorman in their lobby, he said, "Welcome back, Mrs. Bradley." Frank was one of the only people who called her by Spencer's last name. She nodded at him, suddenly realizing how surreal it was to re-enter her life. His words were like a piercing light cutting through the fog, but only for a moment. It was almost as if she was having an out of body experience, as if in a dream state. As they entered their home Chloe ran to the entranceway and hugged Paige tightly. Before she knew it they were all sitting and eating dinner. Gert had made one of Paige's favorites. At first Spencer and Chloe were entirely focused on Paige. They told her about the many cards she had received while she was gone as well as charitable donations made in memory of her father, and they asked her how she was feeling and suggested she take it easy for a while. Soon they were filling her in about work and school. It all sounded like chatter but she did her best to appear present. Saying she was tired, Paige went to bed right after dinner.

When she woke up in the morning it took a few minutes to gather her bearings. *I can't function like this,* she thought to herself. *I have to get back to some routine, some normalcy. Maybe I can forget what I did. People make this mistake all the time and they find a way to function. I have to get back to my routine. God, Spencer and Chloe were so happy to see me. If I can just get back to normal, I can make it up to them. I will be the perfect wife, the perfect mother. I just have to start getting back to my routine. I have mountains to do for the trafficking gala and only a few weeks left. I'll just stay busy to get back on course.* With that thought, Paige got out of bed and back into the structure of daily life.

Although her routine no doubt looked the same to anyone watching, consisting of the normal running, working and family dinners, on the inside Paige was untethered. Suddenly she was looking at her life differently. During dinners where Spencer recounted legal hassles over zoning issues or asked her to clear her schedule for an upcoming business event, Paige wondered how their lives had become scripted. So much of their lives seemed to be determined and their interactions suddenly felt repetitive and sterile. At dinner she would have trouble focusing on what Spencer or Chloe said. She found herself looking around their beautiful home and wondering why she didn't appreciate it more and why she didn't feel connected to her life. She contemplated the things Jake had said to her and how she had sought him out, but as the days rolled on she found herself thinking about him less. After a couple of weeks she started to feel a distance from her time with Jake. She remembered how he had imagined she became an artist and realized how little they knew of each other at this point in their lives. Although she still wondered whether she had chosen her life or it had chosen her, she no longer worried that it was really about Jake, it wasn't. Everyone's busyness coupled with their expectation of her grief allowed her to breath. Spencer was swamped at work, Chloe was barely ever home and she was immersed in the final details of the WIN event.

The night of the WIN gala was Paige's first major public appearance since her father's passing. She wore a simple black evening gown and sapphire earrings. Paige always opted for understated elegance, which was a part of what made her beauty seem so effortless. There was always an odd expectation of glamour at these fundraisers, as if reams of satin and taffeta or flashes from diamonds could somehow lessen the ugliness of the need for events such as these. Spencer had been so overworked lately that Paige gave him the night off and attended on her own, which she preferred when working.

Although there was a huge staff overseeing the final details, Paige arrived an hour early as always to make certain that everything was in order in accord with her specifications. The grand ballroom was stunning, filled with large round tables draped in gold silk and sparkling with candles and fine silver. There were auction tables and charity collection boxes around the perimeter of the room. Behind each station hung a framed poster with images and stories of girls and women who had been helped by WIN and their co-sponsor, Women for Women International. Paige spent some time reading the story of one woman, Gloria, a multiple assault survivor now working to help other women in the conflict zone she calls home. It was very moving.

Soon the place was filled with people dressed in their best and checkbooks in hand. Ashley, Salma, Goldie, Demi and all of the charities' Hollywood heavy hitters had jetted in for the event. The paparazzi snapped shot after shot of their grand entrances, and Paige was hopeful it would translate into some good coverage of the event. In the beginning of the evening everyone Paige greeted offered condolences, and she was forced to repeat things like, "Thank you. Yes, he was a wonderful man. I will miss him terribly," over and over again. Soon the event's master of ceremonies, the founder of WIN, instructed everyone to take their seats. Paige welcomed the start of the special speakers as an opportunity to focus everyone's attention on the cause at hand.

Paige was seated at a table up front along with some of the Hollywood A-listers, the founder of WIN, a woman saved from trafficking in India and her close friend Sarah Cohen, a feminist historian she had met years earlier at a similar event. Paige was seated between Ashley and Sarah. As they listened to the speakers recount grim statistics about kidnapped and prostituted girls and women, Paige began to think about how lucky she was; a kind of luck no one earned and so few had. Soon a woman from Ghana was speaking about her experience as a prostituted woman and the dozen clients she was forced to service six days a week.

Ashley leaned over to Paige and said, "There was a woman I met in Ghana who worked in the same brothel. As you can imagine it was in a horrible neighborhood so her husband took the bus there with her each night and walked her within a block of the place. Then he returned home to care for their two small children while she worked. Can you imagine what that must be like?" she asked.

Paige just shook her head. It was truly unimaginable.

Sarah leaned over, her long curls brushing against Paige's arm, and whispered, "I wonder what she and her husband talk about, at home, both before and after."

"I know, it's amazing what the spirit can survive, and what love can endure," Ashley replied. "I don't think they talk about it. I think they just do what they need to do because it's a matter of survival." Ashley paused and then continued, "Such a tragedy of humanity."

"It must be agony," Paige said. "For both of them, especially if they love each other. It must be torture. And I suppose if they don't love each other, well that must be torture too."

Then Paige started to think about her own life. She wondered if she loved someone enough to survive that with them and if someone loved her that much in return. Like a wave of truth washing over her, it was suddenly so clear. There was only one person she could survive anything with: Spencer. If they were living in that hell, he would swallow his pride and he wouldn't let her take the bus alone, and he wouldn't make her talk about it. He loved her. They loved each other, and their love was real, deep and all their own. They had built it together on adventures and patiently over time. And with the luck of birth, they never had to endure such degradation. They were blessed in ways that no one earns and that shouldn't be wasted.

Suddenly her mind was like a strobe light again, but now it was flashing with images of her life with Spencer and she didn't want it to stop. She remembered hiding under his jacket as they ran from a theatre in the heavy rains of London both giggling uncontrollably; she remembered how he rubbed her forehead with a cold compress in Peru when she became violently ill; she remembered the look on his face when they travelled to Auschwitz and first saw the sheer size of it; she remembered how he would always cut off her mother's snide comments with compliments that Eleanor couldn't resist; she remembered his face as he saw her walking down the aisle towards him and the first time they both saw Chloe. More than anything, she remembered that he was always there for her, and she wanted him to be there. The flashes of his face kept coming. If she had gotten married for the wrong reasons, it didn't matter, she married the right man.

She did her best to say thank you and goodbye to everyone as quickly as she could, eager to get home. When she arrived home she dashed upstairs, feeling free and desperate to see Spencer. She entered the dimly lit main living room to find him sitting on a couch, drinking scotch. Just as she opened her mouth he said, "Aggie sent over a box of papers for you. They're over there," he said pointing to a cardboard box on a side table."

"Oh, Ok," she said as she took off her wrap and flung it on the back of an armchair.

"It's mostly mail. I went through it for you, so you wouldn't have to deal with it."

"Thank you," she said, wondering why he sounded and looked so strange.

"Lots of lovely cards wishing you well. There was also a note from someone named Jake."

Her heart sank, "Oh, I…" but he cut her off.

"Apparently he feels badly. Tell me Paige, why does he feel badly?" he asked, now leaning forward in his chair.

She looked at him, her heart now racing.

"You're not sure? Is it because you fucked him perhaps? Does he feel badly that you screwed?" he shouted as he jumped up and threw the letter towards her.

"Spencer, please I can…"

"Stop!" he shouted. Don't say a word, not one word. I guess now I know why you were in such a rush to send me back to New York."

"No, it wasn't...."

"Stop," he said in an eerily calm voice. "Don't say a word. There is nothing to say. When Chloe moves out we're done," he said as he passed by her.

"Wait," she said, reaching out to touch his shoulder.

He turned and looked at her with an expression of disgust she had never seen before. "You knew about my mother, about what it did to me when my mother fucking killed herself because of my father's infidelity. It was the one thing I told you I could never forgive. You knew from the beginning this was the deal breaker, but..." he paused before continuing, "I will keep up this charade of a marriage for now, but the day Chloe moves out we are done."

He walked out of the room leaving her shocked and unable to move. *What have I done?* repeated in her mind. After a few moments passed she reached down and picked the letter up off of the floor. It read:

Paige,

I'm sorry. I never should have come to the funeral. What you said was right. I knew you were messed up and I should have left you alone. If I loved you I wouldn't want you to screw up your life and I don't. Your husband seems like a standup guy and you should make it work with him. I will never forget our night together. I won't bother you again but if you ever need me I'll be there. If he ever hurts you...

Love,
Jake

She crumpled up the note and threw it in the fireplace.

Over the next couple of weeks Paige and Spencer carried on their work lives, Chloe went to school, and they all sat together at dinner. Unless in the company of others, Spencer did not say one single word to Paige. Although they had many extra bedrooms they continued sharing a room. They never discussed this and Paige didn't know what it meant, if anything. She hoped that despite his pronouncement, Spencer didn't want to make the bridge back to each other any longer. Each night as they lay down to go to sleep Paige thought about saying something to Spencer but his body language was so angry and detached and she didn't know what she could possibly say. Sometimes she opened her mouth to speak but he always turned away, and she let it go. She convinced herself that if enough time passed it would somehow be all right.

During this time Chloe decided that she was either going to go to Stanford or Columbia. Chris, whom she had been madly in love with for the last year and a half, was going to school in California and they had plans to take a road trip across country together. Paige started hoping that Chloe would go to Columbia instead, thinking that if she was still in New York maybe Spencer would reconsider, and she would have more time to work things out with him. Soon, Paige found herself actively hoping that Chloe would be rejected from Stanford and forced to stay in New York by default. She checked the mailbox compulsively waiting for word from Stanford.

Time passed, without change in their lives, and soon it was two months from when Spencer had announced their marriage was over. Paige continued to check the mail religiously.

Part Two

CHAPTER 5

Mollie Johnston's Tuesday morning began just as any other day. She got up at seven o'clock to make coffee and buttered toast for Paul. They sat together, eating toast and trading sections of the *New York Times* until it was time for Paul to leave for work. As always, he brought his dishes to the kitchen sink and then returned to the table to give Mollie a quick kiss goodbye. "Have a great day. I love you," he said as he picked up his briefcase and walked out the door. As Mollie locked the door behind him she grabbed the latest *People Magazine* from the stand by the door and returned to the table for a second cup of coffee. She then unloaded the dishwasher from the night before and reloaded it with their breakfast mugs and plates.

After her morning shower she wiped the steamed up bathroom mirror with her hand and stared at herself, noticing, per usual, that her pores were too large. No matter what creams or treatments she tried they were too big. She applied a thick layer of foundation and pressed powder to try to conceal her unsightly pores. Next was the job of trying to groom her unruly hair. If the curls around her face didn't dry in just the right way she was bothered all day. Most days they didn't dry correctly but on this day she was lucky. Mollie felt good as she left the bathroom to pick an outfit from her closet but the feeling soon passed as she looked at the clothes hanging before her. She hated her clothes. She thought that she should really buy new clothes for her new life in the city but had promised Paul she would be frugal. More than that, she didn't want to buy anything until she lost weight. Now that she belonged to the health club she had no excuses. *I will lose weight. I will lose weight,* played over and over again in her mind as she looked at her reflection in the mirror. Finally settling on a pair of jeggings and a loose cowl neck sweater in her favorite shade of indigo, she went back to the mirror for a final onceover. Soon she found herself standing as close to the mirror as possible, again examining the pores on her face. *Maybe I should try that new minimizer,* she thought to herself. She went back to the magazine stand to retrieve the *People* magazine again and flipped through it looking for the cosmetics insert. When she found the right page she tore it out, slipped it into her handbag, put on her coat and left.

After running her normal errands—picking up some toiletries for Paul and stopping at the Post Office to return some DVDs and buy stamps— she decided to stroll down Fifth Avenue. Whenever she didn't know what to do with herself, she walked down Fifth Avenue—it was her favorite place. Mindful of her budgetary issues she never bought anything more than a couple of chocolates, magazines or an inexpensive Pashmina scarf from a street vendor (which she usually sent to a relative as a gift). Sometimes she bought Paul a special pastry or piece of marzipan for dessert. If she was hungry she grabbed a hotdog or pretzel from a cart, sat on a stoop and thought about how lucky she was to live there.

On this day she decided to go to Bergdorf Goodman to try to get a sample of the product she had seen in the magazine. She never bought anything in Bergdorf's but she enjoyed visiting the high-end cosmetic counter because they handed out the best samples. When she had made her way down Fifth to Bergdorf's she walked in with purpose, and headed straight to cosmetics, stopping to pick up a sample of Chanel No. 5 on route. As she waited at the cosmetic counter she heard, "Mollie, Mollie is that you darling?" Thinking it couldn't possibly be directed at her, she ignored it until the voice got louder, "Why it is you."

She turned to see Gwen approaching wearing a full-length gold trench coat and carrying a matching Fendi bag. "Oh, hi Gwen," Mollie said happily. "How are you?"

"Oh, you know, I am just mad with errands," she said as she rolled her eyes and then leaned in to air kiss Mollie's cheek. "Have you seen Paige lately? I left two messages for her and no word."

Before Mollie could respond the woman behind the cosmetic counter interrupted, "Can I help you Ma'am?" she asked Mollie. Flustered, Mollie said, "Oh, yes, you have a product I wanted to try," and then lowering her voice, "It's a pore minimizer."

Gwen grabbed a tester bottle off of the counter and said, "This, right dear? It's fabulous. You should get the large. The small will be gone in a flash."

"Uh, well..." Mollie stumbled, wondering if Gwen was noticing how large her pores were or if she was implying her face was big too.

"Wrap it up for her, please," Gwen directed the saleswoman.

Mollie took her wallet out of her bag and slid her credit card through the machine. She tried to hide her sticker shock when she saw the price. *It's Ok. I never splurge and I really need this and it must be good if Gwen knows it,* she rationalized.

As she took the small shopping bag she turned to Gwen and said, "Thank you for your help."

"Well now you can return the favor, come up to shoes with me. I have to find something for an event this weekend and I need a second opinion, unless you're in a rush."

Gwen started walking off before Mollie could answer so Mollie just followed her. An hour later Gwen was buying two pairs of designer shoes that cost nearly as much as Mollie's rent. "Shall we go to lunch?" Gwen asked.

"Oh, sure, that would be great," Mollie said both surprised and thrilled by the invitation.

Mollie followed Gwen out of Bergdorf's and onto the bustling street. She tried to keep up as Gwen headed down Fifth with determination, quickly entering a store and then up an escalator that took them to an ultra-modern restaurant overlooking Fifth Avenue. The host escorted them to a circular booth by a window. Mollie sat down on the white leather and looked around at the Euro-chic décor. It was a lot to take in and unlike anyplace she had ever been. As the host handed them their menus Gwen said, "A bottle of Pellegrino please."

Mollie opened her menu and said, "Oh, I love Italian food. What do you normally have here?"

"Carpaccio and an arugula salad, unless they have a tuna Carpaccio special, then sometimes I have that. Do you know what you want?" she asked, signaling to the waiter.

"Oh," Mollie said, startled when the waiter popped over so quickly. "I'll have the Carpaccio and the arugula salad, but light on the parmesan and olive oil on the side," Gwen said, smiling as she handed her menu to him.

"And for you Miss?"

"What is the risotto special?"

"Chicken and asparagus with a little truffle oil. It's very delicious."

"I'll have that, please."

"Very good," he said, taking her menu.

"Oh how I envy you," Gwen said.

Mollie smiled awkwardly. "Darling I need to run to the ladies room, I'll be back in a flash," Gwen said as she excused herself.

As Mollie sat waiting for Gwen she looked around at the other people in the restaurant. Everyone there looked as if they had stepped out of the pages of a magazine. There were shopping bags from Bergdorf's or Bendel's at every table and Fendi, Hermes and Chanel handbags gently placed on table tops or on extra chairs, as if they too were guests of the restaurant. While there were some people in suits who looked like they were on business lunches, they were the exception. She felt terribly out of place thinking to herself, *I must look so out of step with Gwen. I bet the waiter is wondering why we're here together. When she comes back will we have anything to talk about? I hope Paul isn't mad when he sees the credit card bill.* Soon her stream of consciousness turned into a pep talk. *Now stop that Mollie, she invited me and I'm a people person. I can make new friends. And I belong here just like anyone else. Paul made this move so I could see places like this so I should just enjoy it. I...* but her thoughts were interrupted as Gwen returned, followed by the waiter who delivered a basket of focaccia.

As Mollie took a piece of focaccia Gwen asked, "So have you spoken to Paige lately?"

"Not since we all had lunch. How did you and Paige meet?"

"Oh we met years ago at a party at The MET. Actually, this dreadful woman, Barbara, a social climber if I ever saw one, well she cornered Paige at the shellfish table and I could see poor Paige was trapped, she's so polite. So I turned to them and said 'Oh darling, there you are. Come and say hello to Redmond,' and she was able to escape that awful woman."

"And you had never met?" Mollie asked in disbelief.

"No, never. Although of course we discovered we had many mutual acquaintances. But needless to say after she thanked me for rescuing her we had a good chuckle and became fast friends. Paige being Paige invited me to lunch the next week and that was it."

"That's a fantastic story," Mollie said.

Gwen smiled. "Yes, well, seems so long ago now. Something is going on with her these days, I think." She shook her head and said, "She was very close with her father, I think she may be depressed."

"It's understandable. It sounds like it had been quite a shock. And well, you're never quite ready to let go of the people you love, are you?" Mollie asked.

Gwen shook her head.

With that the waiter delivered their food and they started eating. "My father-in-law died several years ago, from cancer, and gosh it took Paul more than a year to be back to himself. It's very hard."

Gwen nodded and the two continued talking through lunch as well as two rounds of cappuccinos. When the waiter delivered the check Gwen grabbed it. "Oh, please let's share it," Mollie protested.

"Nonsense. I invited you and I owe you for being so patient while I tried on shoe after shoe," she said with a smile as she handed the waiter her credit card.

"Well thank you. This was great. You never told me, what is the event you needed the shoes for?"

"There's a special opening at the Whitney this Friday night for major contributors, blah, blah, blah. I need to show my face. Actually, I'm nearly certain Paige and Spencer will be there. Why don't you join us?"

"Oh, no I didn't mean..." but Gwen cut her off. "Please, do come. You can meet some people and I'd just love to meet your husband. It's at seven o'clock but no need to rush. Dress for a cocktail party. Will you come?"

Mollie nodded. "We'd love to, thank you. Do we need tickets or something?"

Gwen smirked. "No darling, don't worry about a thing. You will be on the list." Then she handed Mollie her phone and said, "Put your number in and I'll give you mine." After exchanging phone numbers they stood up, collected their bags and took the escalator down. When they reached the lobby of the store Gwen leaned in to give Mollie a peck on the cheek. "Look forward to seeing you Friday. I have to run."

"Bye," Mollie shouted as Gwen darted outside.

*

Upon arriving at home Gwen immediately slipped her shopping bag into the hallway closet. Then she went into the kitchen to get some water. When she tried to use the ice-maker on the refrigerator door it made a clunking noise and began leaking. The water dripped down the sleeve of her coat. "Damn," she whispered. "It's still broken," she continued as she ripped a paper towel to dry her arm and wipe what had leaked onto the floor. She threw away the paper towel and walked over to the study and knocked on the door. "Yes," she heard her husband say.

"Hi dear, the ice-maker is still broken."

He shrugged.

"Well I'd like to get it fixed. Do you know where the service contract is?" she asked, staring at him.

He shrugged. "Don't you have someplace we keep those things, Gwen?"

"Abby always took care of those things for me."

He shrugged again.

"Any news from Donald?" she asked.

He shook his head.

"Well, I'll leave you to it then. Shall I go around the corner and pick up a roast chicken or something for dinner?"

He nodded and just as she was leaving the room he said, "I may have to go out for a bit later."

She squeezed her eyes shut for a moment and continued out of the room, closing the door behind her.

*

When Paul arrived home that evening he was greeted by his wife even more exuberantly than usual. Before he had put down his briefcase or taken off his coat Mollie was already talking a mile a minute from the kitchen "Honey, honey is that you?" continuing before he could answer, "You'll never believe who I ran into today, Gwen McAndrews. You remember I had told you about her, Paige's friend Gwen."

"Uh huh," he said as he came up and gave her a peck on the head. "That smells good," he said taking a whiff of the roasted pork chops and vegetables cooling on the counter.

"Dinner will be ready in a minute. I have so much to tell you."

"Well Ok, sounds good. Let me go take off my tie and wash up and I'll be right back."

Minutes later Mollie and Paul were eating dinner. "So, you bumped into Paige's friend Gwen?" he asked as he dunked a piece of pork into the apple sauce on his plate.

"Yes. I was in a department store waiting at a cosmetics counter and the next thing you know Gwen was there and I helped her do a little shopping and then we went out for lunch."

"Well that sounds nice, where did you go?"

"Some Italian place on top of the Armani store on Fifth Avenue. You should have seen the view and oh my god, the food was so good. But what I want to tell you," but before she could continue he asked, "What does Gwen do? Does she work?"

"Her husband is a businessman. I'm not sure exactly what he does but he's very successful. They live on Park Avenue, I guess near Paige and Spencer. I know that when she met her husband she was a well-known realtor in Manhattan but I don't think she does that anymore. I don't really know. Maybe she does charity stuff or something like Paige."

"Do they have kids?"

"No, they don't have any kids. But Honey, the best part was that they invited us to an event at the Whitney Museum this Friday night," she said, as she scooped some more carrots from the serving dish and placed them on Paul's plate.

"Well that's nice," he said. "What is the event for?"

"Oh I don't know. Something for benefactors or something. Anyway, Gwen said Paige and Spencer will be there too. Can we go?"

"Of course we can go. I'll leave work a little early to make sure I'm home in plenty of time."

Mollie was beaming ear to ear, and the two continued eating. A few minutes later she said, "I don't know what I'm going to wear. I mean I was thinking you could wear your nice charcoal suit but I looked through my closet and I just don't know."

"I'm sure you'll look beautiful no matter what you wear. Is it very dressy?"

"Gwen said to dress for a cocktail party but you know how New York is, everything is dressy and these people are always ultra-chic."

"Well if you need to, just go buy yourself something."

"Oh, I know we're trying not to spend too much," she said.

As he continued eating his dinner he said, "Treat yourself. See if you can find a nice new dress."

"Oh, well, I'll see… can I get you another chop?" she asked.

"This is plenty, thanks for making one of my favorites."

She smiled and they continued talking about his day and their boys and making other chatter.

After clearing the dishes together they sat on the couch and watched their favorite sitcoms. Paul nearly toppled over from laughter a few times, causing Mollie to tease him. Soon they got ready for bed. Paul drifted to sleep right after they made love, but Mollie lay awake for hours replaying her day.

CHAPTER 6

Friday night Paul walked in the door at six o'clock sharp. When he didn't receive his normal greeting from Mollie, he called, "Honey, are you here?"

"I'm in the bedroom," she shouted. He walked into their bedroom to find Mollie frantically scouring her jewelry box, wearing only a bra, slip and pantyhose.

"Hi, Honey," he said, placing his briefcase beside the bed.

"Hi. I'm not ready and I can't talk. Your charcoal suit is hanging in the dry cleaning bag on the closet door. I had it pressed. I put a nice tie and shirt there too."

"I'll change right away. What time do you want to leave?"

"It starts at seven but Gwen said people don't arrive right on time. I think we should plan to be there at a quarter past. It could be tough getting a cab so we need to plan for that."

"Ok," he said.

Paul dressed quickly and went to watch TV in the living room while he waited.

Now in the bathroom, still partly dressed, Mollie was touching up her makeup when she noticed that her hair still hadn't set right. She knew that morning after drying it that it wasn't right but hoped it would fall into place by night; sometimes that happened. As she tried to reposition the curls around her face, she berated herself for not rewashing it when she still had time. Desperate, she took a couple of Bobbi pins and tried to fix it. She thought it looked better, but not great. She put on her diamond stud earrings, her tenth anniversary gift from Paul, and a touch more powder before returning to her bedroom to dress. She got a bit tangled as she tried to put on her new black wrap dress. She finally had it adjusted correctly but after a look in her full-length mirror she decided to wear the higher waist Spanx underneath. After making the switch she grabbed her evening bag and walked into the living room. When she saw Paul eating pretzels she said, "What are you doing? They're serving food there. And oh my god, look at you, you have crumbs."

79

He started wiping the couple errant crumbs from his chest. "I thought it might be a while until we have something to eat and I was hungry. It was just a snack." Then he paused for a moment and said, "Wow, you look great."

"Oh, do you think I look Ok? My hair didn't come out right but I think I fixed it."

"You look beautiful, like you always do. I like the new dress, very sexy," he said with a smile.

"I tried on so many things but I think this is Ok," she said as she brushed the bottom of the skirt, as if there were wrinkles to smooth away.

Paul stood up to leave but Mollie said, "I think I'll just go to the bathroom one more time," so he sat down again. Moments later they were heading out and soon they were pulling up to the Whitney.

As they had left a few minutes earlier than planned, easily hailed a cab and had good luck with the lights, they arrived at just a few minutes past seven. When they walked up to the door and were asked if they were on the list, Mollie replied, "Yes, we're Mr. and Mrs. Johnston."

The man scoured the list and then said, "I'm sorry but I don't see you. Do you have your invitation?"

"No," Mollie said feeling terribly self-conscious, "We were invited by a friend. Please look again. It's Mollie and Paul Johnston."

As he checked the list again, shaking his head, she added, "We're guests of Gwen McAndrews."

He flipped to another page and exclaimed, "Ah, there you are. I apologize for the delay." He opened the door and said, "Have a wonderful evening," as they walked in. Inside they were greeted by a woman who pointed them to the coat check, from where they were directed downstairs to what was normally the café area but tonight was set up for a party with white table cloths, votive candles and small bouquets of hydrangea. They were the first to arrive, and the only other people down there were staff, which again left Mollie feeling over-exposed. A waiter immediately offered them champagne or water. Mollie took a glass of champagne and then asked Paul to hold it while she went to the ladies room. When she returned they stood and made small talk about how pretty the room was as they watched guests slowly trickle in. Twenty five minutes later they saw Paige and Spencer walking down the stairs. Mollie thought Paige looked stunning. Paige was wearing an above-the-knee black crepe dress with a cap sleeve and a sleek patent leather belt and nude Manolo Blahnik pumps and she was carrying a black clutch under one arm. Her only jewelry consisted of large emerald earrings and a matching cocktail ring that Mollie couldn't get over. Spencer was in a black suit and together they looked like Hollywood royalty.

Mollie and Paul smiled and Paige nodded and walked straight over to them. Paige leaned in and gave Mollie a little hug as she said, "It's wonderful to see you, Gwen mentioned you were coming."

Mollie smiled and said, "You remember my husband Paul?"

"Yes, of course," Paige said as she shook his hand. "It's nice to see you again, thank you for coming. And you both remember Spencer."

They all nodded, shook hands and said hello. Then Paige asked, "Has Gwen arrived yet?"

"No, not yet," Mollie said.

"Gwen likes to make a grand entrance, which requires being late," Spencer said sarcastically. Paige rolled her eyes and smiled before conceding, "Well it is true, she's never on time for anything."

They all smiled. When the waiter passed by, Spencer took a glass of champagne for himself and a water for Paige. They stood and chatted about the museum and other museums in New York as waiters started passing around Hors D'oeuvres such as tiny goat cheese and fig tartlets, brioche crostini with duck confit, fried oysters and rosemary baby lamb chops that Paul couldn't get enough of. Before long all heads turned as Gwen and Redmond walked in. Gwen was decked out in a gold sequined top, black slacks and a large gold cuff bracelet. Her lips were fire engine red and a clutch that looked like it was made of blocks of gold was tucked under one arm. Punctuated by her platinum blonde hair, it was impossible not to notice her. She immediately joined the group and introduced Redmond to Mollie and Paul. When she met Paul she gave him a half hug but he was holding a glass in one hand and a napkin with a crostini in the other and couldn't quite reciprocate. Mollie took note of the awkward exchange. "Well, what have I missed?" Gwen asked, grabbing a glass of champagne from a passing waiter.

"The food is just delicious," Mollie said.

"The lamb chops are amazing. Keep your eyes open if they pass those around again," Paul added.

Gwen smirked, and Mollie gave Paul a glance that implied she was displeased. "Uh, thank you so much for inviting us," Paul said cheerfully.

"Our pleasure," Gwen said.

Mollie thought she heard Redmond sigh but she wasn't sure. Gwen rubbed his arm a moment later like she was consoling him, which made Mollie think he had in fact sighed. She wondered if he was upset that Gwen had invited them.

Wanting nothing more than to fit in Mollie said, "You look beautiful, Gwen."

Gwen smiled as everyone nodded in agreement and Mollie added, "You're not wearing the shoes you bought."

Redmond gave Gwen a sideways look, and Mollie sensed that she had said something wrong.

"Oh, I decided to wear slacks instead of the dress I was planning on so you know how it is, you change one thing and you have to change it all."

She laughed, and almost everyone followed her lead.

Soon it was eight o'clock, and they were invited up into one of the galleries for a special showing and talk. When they returned downstairs half an hour later they were escorted to their table and immediately served a salad that Mollie thought looked too pretty to eat. Thinly sliced English cucumbers encircled a beautiful green salad topped with bright orange edible flowers. "I think these are nasturtium blossoms," Mollie said to the group. "They were Isabella Stewart Gardner's favorite flower. They only bloom for a few weeks but the blossoms are edible." Everyone seemed impressed. Paul immediately removed the flowers from his salad, placing them on his bread plate, which Mollie wished he hadn't done. A waiter came by offering everyone a choice of white or red wine. Mollie and Paul chose red and the others white, except for Redmond who just had sparkling water.

"So, Mollie, what did you think of that exhibit? I'm dying to get your art-eye perspective," Paige said as she sliced into a cucumber.

Suddenly all eyes were on Mollie. She tried to chew the food in her mouth quickly before responding, "I thought it was very interesting, and a real treat to see before the public. I saw a lot of Kandinsky's influence in the larger pieces and I really liked the textural elements."

Paige nodded as Redmond asked, "Are you an artist or a dealer?"

Mollie laughed. "Oh no, neither really. I studied art in college but it was never a career or anything. I'm sure I don't really know what I'm talking about. What did all of you think of the exhibit?"

"Now you're just way too modest," Paul chimed in. "Mollie studied fine arts in college and she's very talented."

Mollie blushed and said, "Oh, Paul is just biased."

"He's right," Paige added. "You were always naturally talented and you had the best eye. When we had our art history exams we had to identify slide after slide and Mollie always just breezed through it."

"Is that how you two met?" Gwen asked.

"Yes," Paige said. "We had several art history classes together. If I remember correctly, Mollie didn't even have to take them, she elected to."

"I remember how you used to study for those slide tests," Spencer said, turning to Paige and smiling. "It was just awful. You always over studied, became confused and then got frustrated with me when I quizzed you."

"I did not," she protested.

"You absolutely did, it was brutal," he said with a laugh.

"Well it couldn't have been worse than all of your flashcards with the scribbles," Paige said with a giggle. "Spencer always wrote his study cards so quickly that later he could barely read them and when I quizzed him I never had any idea if he actually gave the right answer so I just nodded and moved on."

"I *knew* you were doing that," he said, playfully brushing his shoulder on hers. The two laughed and everyone joined in.

"So Mollie, what kinds of art did you make? Did you have a medium you specialized in?" Gwen asked.

"Sculpture. I dabbled with just about every medium at one time or another, but I really loved working with clay."

"You should see the beautiful sculptures we have! They're incredible," Paul said.

Mollie looked down and shook her head ever so slightly.

"Do you still sculpt, Mollie?" Gwen asked.

"Not as much as I'd like to, but I hope to do more now that I have the time. There is a studio a couple of blocks from the health club actually and I thought I might go sometime. They allow drop-ins so…"

"I've seen that place," Paige said. "I've always been curious about it."

"Well maybe you'd like to go sometime," Mollie said.

"Oh, I'm just so busy with work and I don't know how to do anything anyway," Paige said.

"It's never too late to learn, right?" Paul said.

"Well, if you ever want to go just let me know," Mollie said.

Paige smiled politely, and not a moment later the wait staff came over and cleared their salad plates and began serving a beautiful poached salmon dinner.

*

"That was a wonderful night," Mollie said from the edge of the bed, as she unrolled her pantyhose.

"Uh huh," Paul replied as he hung up his suit. "I'm glad you had a good time."

"Well didn't you have a good time?"

"Yes, I did. I thought it was very cool," he said somewhat defensively. "I know how much you were looking forward to it,

84

that's all I meant." Returning to the bedroom he added, "It was wild to see Paige and Spencer after all these years."

"They look amazing, don't they?"

"Uh huh," he said, as he perched a couple of pillows behind his back to read in bed while he waited for Mollie.

"Paige was really impressed with your artistic eye and talent."

"Oh, I was so embarrassed. I'm sure she was just being polite but honestly, I wish you wouldn't have gone on about it," Mollie said, now making her way to the bathroom to finish getting ready for bed.

"Are you kidding? She remembered not only what you studied in college but how good you were at it after twenty years. I don't think I remember that about anyone. You shouldn't diminish yourself. She was genuinely impressed. I really think you should start sculpting more now that you're in the art center of the world."

Mollie spit her toothpaste out and hollered back, "She always had a great memory."

By this time Paul had given up and started reading.

Soon Mollie got into bed and said, "Gwen is so glamorous don't you think?"

"Well, she's certainly done up," he said, still reading his book.

"She's sophisticated. And it was so kind of her to invite us, don't you think?"

"Uh huh, it was very nice of her." Then he looked up from his book and said, "Her husband didn't say a word all night other than asking what you do. I thought that was strange especially considering they're good friends with Paige and Spencer."

"Well, maybe he's shy."

Paul gave her a look and shook his head. "I don't think a man like that, and married to a woman like that, suffers from shyness." He then laughed like he was proud of what he had said before continuing, "It seemed like something was wrong with him."

"Maybe he had a long day and was tired."

"Maybe," Paul acquiesced.

"Do you think he didn't like us?" Mollie asked. "Do you think he was upset that Gwen invited us?"

"No, not at all. That never crossed my mind. I'm sure it had nothing to do with us. It just seemed like he was, um, I don't know, far off. I was just wondering what kind of marriage they have but you're probably right, most likely he was tired or something."

"I did think he gave Gwen a look about me at one point, did you see that?" Mollie asked.

"No, and I'm sure it's nothing like that at all. I'm sorry I said anything. It was a fun night and I'd be happy to go out with them again. And it was nice of Paige and Gwen to invite you to meet them at the gym tomorrow too. It seems like they could become good friends. Let's get some sleep," he said as he leaned over and gave her a peck.

"Goodnight, Honey," he said as he turned the light off.

"Goodnight," she said. As Mollie tried to fall asleep, she found herself wondering if she really could become good friends with Paige and Gwen.

*

The next morning Paige woke up long before Spencer. She had barely slept, replaying the night in her head. At moments it had felt like old times, for the first time in what seemed like forever. He had joked with her, teased her, laughed and even touched her. She wondered, *What did it mean? Is he forgiving me? Are we moving on?* These questions were met with equally gnawing doubts like: *I'm just seeing what I want to see. He's just pretending for the sake of appearances.* Soon her thoughts were interrupted as Spencer sighed and rumbled around a bit. He stretched his arms up before sitting up, back turned to her, and walking straight into their bathroom. She wanted desperately to get up and say something to him, but she didn't know what to say and she was afraid of derailing any progress they were making. If things were getting better, she didn't want to do anything to set them back. As she began to sit up she heard the shower and knew the moment was gone. She got out of bed and put her running clothes on. As she laced her sneakers she heard the shower stop but she decided to go for her run before Spencer came out of the bathroom.

On her way out she stopped to use the powder room in the hallway. As she dried her hands she stopped to rub her fingers across the border of the lace hand towels, remembering when they had bought them in Bruges. They had just shared a sugar waffle from a street vendor, something entirely off her normal diet because Spencer said, "Just live a little. I'll share it with you." Then it started to sprinkle, and they had run into a tourist store to duck for cover where they ended up buying lace embroidered hand towels. Their shared laughter the night before at the Whitney popped into her mind again and she thought, *it can't be an act.*

After her run she stopped at home and looked around for Spencer, hoping to spend a few minutes with him and gauge if it might be the right time to talk. He was nowhere to be found so she grabbed her gym bag and headed out to meet Gwen and Mollie.

As soon as she arrived at the gym she headed to the locker room where she bumped into Mollie. "Hi, Mollie. How are you?"

"Good. Last night was so much fun, Paul and I really enjoyed the event."

Paige smiled. "It was nice to see Paul again. He looks well. And he's just so crazy about you. It's wonderful to see how well things have turned out for you."

Mollie smiled. "Thank you. And gosh, you and Spencer are just as I remembered."

Paige smiled silently wondering. *Were we unhappy back then too, or happy? Or is it just that we look the same, because Spencer is pretending? Is there really no difference to people between us then and now?*

At that moment Gwen walked in, "Good morning ladies. Paige, I hope you weren't waiting long. I went for a seaweed wrap this morning and let's just say it took longer to unwrap me than expected," she said with a laugh.

Mollie laughed too.

"I just got here," Paige said.

"What's a seaweed wrap like?" Mollie asked Gwen.

"Oh darling, they're fabulous. They take all the toxins out. I normally pair it with a facial but I just didn't have the time. But you can't go just anywhere. You have to go to Deluxe on Madison. Of course you pay a premium but you can't put a price on clear pores. Oh, and you can have a mani-pedi done while you have the body treatments. I do love multi-tasking. I can get you an appointment if you decide to try it."

"Oh, thanks Gwen. I was just curious really," Mollie said.

Gwen shrugged and said, "Well ladies, after that dinner last night I think we could all use a good sweat."

"I'm going to take a Pilates class while you two play," Mollie said as she picked up her water bottle and towel.

Looking at Gwen, Paige said, "I need to put my things in my locker. I'll meet you on the court in a few," and then turning to Mollie she added, "Enjoy Pilates. We'll meet you back here after our game."

Two hours later, all freshly showered and dressed, the women were ordering brunch. Although, per usual, Paige and Gwen had their regular orders, they held onto their menus long enough for Mollie to have a chance to decide what she wanted. As they passed their menus to the waiter Gwen said, "So ladies, what are your plans for the rest of the weekend?"

"Paul mentioned a movie he wanted to see so I think we might do that. I've been looking for an excuse to go to the Paris Theater."

"It's a great theater," Paige said.

"And so close to Bergies," Gwen said with a smile.

"What about you two?" Mollie asked, as she picked up a pecan sticky bun from the bread basket. Before anyone responded Mollie muttered, "Why do I always eat these?"

"What did you say, dear?" Gwen asked.

Realizing she had drawn unwanted attention to herself she said, "Oh, I just have such a weakness for pecan or cinnamon rolls, anything in the stickybun family. I've been promising myself to watch what I eat but..." she trailed off before adding, "Paul tells me to just enjoy myself but how happy will he be when I'm enormous?"

As she put the uneaten bun down on her bread plate Gwen said, "Well if you really want to make a change I know a wonderful nutritionist who can get you on a program. And the personal trainers at the club are fabulous."

Mollie smiled and Paige said, "I think it's lovely that Paul just wants you to enjoy yourself. He seems like such a supportive person."

"Uh, yes. I guess he is," Mollie said.

"Just this morning I was thinking about a trip Spencer and I took years ago. We were in Belgium in this very picturesque, fairy-tale sort of town, and we smelled the most wonderful smell from a small cart, you know a street vendor's cart. He was selling sugar waffles and they were only two euros for plain and three for chocolate. Spencer convinced me to split one with him and god, I'll never forget how delicious it was." Her voice softer, Paige continued, "Funny how just this morning I was thinking of this, not the waffle but, but what I felt sharing it with him."

Gwen's jaw dropped. Paige was not sentimental nor did she ever eat pastries, let alone off of a cart in the street.

"It's funny the things that mean a lot to us," Mollie said warmly.

"Yes, yes it is," Paige responded. "I think it's really lovely that Paul just wants you to be happy. I'm sure that's what gives him joy."

Mollie smiled.

Gwen, with her mouth still wide open, shook her head and said, "Anyway, Mollie, if you ever decide to get serious about a food plan I will get you a name."

Paige shook her head and said, "You know even Gwen has her weaknesses."

Gwen shrugged it off and Mollie smiled and said, "So, you two never said what you're doing this weekend."

They both looked down.

"Oh, nothing special," Gwen said quietly.

"Spencer and I are both swamped at work and Chloe is never home anymore. I think I'll just work for the rest of the weekend, loads to do for the breast cancer event."

Just then their food was served and they began to eat.

At the end of their meal Gwen pulled a red Yves Saint Laurent lipstick and a jeweled hand mirror out of her handbag. As the waiter started clearing the table she said, "I'll have a non-fat cappuccino," before opening her mirror. As the waiter reached for the bread basket Paige said, "Wait," and pulled out a pecan sticky bun. Gwen was so surprised she smeared her lipstick and promptly excused herself so she could fix it. Paige put the bun on her bread plate, cut it in half and held the plate out and Mollie took a half. As Paige bit into her piece of the sweet treat all of the intense feelings of love she had for Spencer that day in Bruges were transposed onto the present. She unwittingly smiled and Mollie said, "It's delicious, isn't it?"

Paige nodded.

Gwen returned, picked up her waiting cappuccino and took a quick sip. "I've taken care of the check ladies, and I have to run. I have an errand for Redomnd." She leaned down and gave them each a peck on the cheek and was off.

A moment later Paige said, "Well, I should go too. I need to get some work done."

"If you need any help with the benefit please let me know. I'd be happy to pitch in."

"Thank you, Mollie. Have a wonderful time at The Paris and I'm sure we'll talk soon. If the week gets away from me I do hope you'll meet us again next Saturday."

Mollie nodded and Paige leaned in and gave her a hug before heading out, with her ponytail with one perfect curl bobbing up and down as she walked away.

When Paige got home she felt grounded for the first time in ages. She was so much lighter that she headed upstairs without checking the mail. Just as she opened the front door, Chloe came running up to her holding some papers in one hand and screaming, "I got in, I got in. Can you believe it? I'm going to California."

She embraced Paige who was still standing in the doorway, arms by her sides and mouth open.

*

When Gwen got home she made a beeline to the walk-in closet in her bedroom. She looked at the rows of dresses and stacks of designer shoe boxes on her side, mirrored by Redmond's suits on the other side, arranged beautifully from the lightest gray to the darkest blues and eventually black. Once an oasis, the closet had become Pandora's Box. She walked to the back and removed the framed *Breakfast at Tiffany's* poster, revealing the safe mounted in the wall. A few clicks and she was pulling out boxes of her jewels. She stacked the boxes carefully on one of the ottomans in the center of the room and sat down on the seat beside the pile. As she opened each box she remembered the times Redmond had surprised her or instances of picking out something special on their many travels. In some cases she simply recalled the last time she wore the piece, and how much fun she and Redmond had getting dressed up and 'taking the town by storm' as they always said. Although she knew when they married there was gossip about her doing it for the money, it was never about money. Redmond made her feel larger than life. He was the smartest, most distinguished person she had ever met and being with him fueled her with invincibility.

Now, looking around the enormous closet once more, she felt sick to her stomach. After returning family heirlooms, anniversary and holiday gifts to the safe and re-hanging the poster, she grabbed the remaining boxes of formerly under-appreciated treasures. She stuck them in a large Stella McCartney bag and walked out of the closet, shutting the doors behind her. On her way out she passed by the study and noticed the door was ajar. She tapped the door open and popped her head in to see Redmond sitting in his favorite chair in the corner, staring out the large window before him.

"Redmond, Redmond dear," she called softly.

He turned his head and she continued, "I'm going out to do an errand. I'll pick up something for dinner on the way home."

He blinked as if to indicate he heard her.

"How are you feeling today?" she asked.

He shrugged before saying, "I may have to go out for a bit later, so if I'm not here when you get back..." he trailed off as she smiled and nodded.

"Well if you're not home I'll keep dinner warm."

He turned around to face the window, and she pulled the door closed, squeezing her eyes tightly for a moment before heading out.

*

As Gwen stood at the counter in one of the finest estate jewelry stores in the city, she thought about how strange it was to feel so out of place in this of all places. She fidgeted with her hair and repositioned her bag from one arm to the other, wishing Mr. Simmons would return from the back with her paperwork and his assessment. While focused on the door to the backroom she heard a voice from behind her say, "Gwen. Gwen is that you?"

She turned to see Paul Johnston smiling at her. "Oh, hello Paul," she said in a startled manner.

"What a small world. Did you see Mollie earlier?" he asked.

Suddenly aware of a tingling sensation coursing through her body, Gwen hesitated before replying, "Yes, yes I did. We had a gal's brunch earlier with Paige. Uh, what brings you here?"

Before he could answer a salesman emerged from the back and asked, "How can I help you?"

"I think she was first," Paul said, indicating to Gwen.

"Oh I'm already being helped by Mr. Simmons," she said to the man.

"Very good. Can I help you Sir?" he said returning his attention to Paul.

"Yes, I'm picking up a ring that was being repaired," Paul replied as he pulled a slip out of his pocket and handed it to the man.

"Thank you, Sir. I'll just be a moment," he said before heading to the back.

"So, you're picking something up?" Gwen asked.

"A ring. Mollie loves antique opals. Her favorite grandmother was crazy about them so I think she associates them with her. When Tom and Jack were born I gave her an antique ring with two oval shaped opals. Last time she wore it she bumped her hand and one of the opals shattered. They're very fragile."

"Hmm, most things are," Gwen interjected.

"Anyway, she was so upset and convinced that the ring would never be the same so I snuck it out of her jewelry box and brought it here quite a while ago and they called this morning to say they found a perfect match and replaced it. I wanted to surprise her with it tonight."

"Well that's lovely, just lovely," Gwen said.

At that moment the salesman returned and presented Paul with a ring box. He opened the box and smiled. "It's Perfect. You did a great job! Thank you!"

Gwen leaned over to peak and said, "It's a beautiful ring."

As Paul took out his wallet to pay, Mr. Simmons emerged from the back with a manila folder filled with papers. He leaned over the counter and handed it to Gwen. "So Mrs. McAndrews, all of the appraisal documents and..." but before he could finish she cleared her throat loudly, cutting him off. "Uh well yes, I'm sure it's all in order. I'll look through it at home and I'll be in touch. I do appreciate your assistance."

He nodded and Gwen tucked the folder into her bag and turned to Paul. "Well I really ought to go. Good luck with your surprise for Mollie."

Paul was just signing the sales slip but looked up to say, "Thank you." Gwen was half way out the door by the time he was able to get out, "Good to see you."

When Paul arrived home Mollie was in their bedroom changing to go out to dinner and a movie.

"Hi, Honey," he called as he approached their room.

"Hi, what have you been up to?" she asked as he walked over and gave her a peck.

"I had an errand and actually you'll never guess who I bumped into."

"Who?"

"Gwen."

"Gwen? That's so funny because I saw her earlier today."

"I know."

"Where did you see her?"

"Weeeeell," he said as he pulled a small box out of his pocket. "Here," he said, handing it to her.

She opened the box and exclaimed, "Oh my goodness. I can't believe it! I just can't believe it! It's a perfect match."

She took the ring out and slipped it on, admiring how it looked on her hand. "How did you do this?"

"I asked around at work and someone recommended an estate jeweler uptown."

"Thank you so much," she said as she gave him a big hug. "So, is that where you saw Gwen, at the jeweler?"

"Yeah, but I got the feeling she wasn't happy to see me."

"Why?" Mollie asked, with her facial expression changing. "What did you say to her?"

"Nothing. I just got the feeling maybe she didn't want anyone to see her there. I think she may have been selling something."

Paul walked into the bathroom to wash his hands as Mollie called after him, "Well, why would you think that?"

"She seemed anxious," he hollered. "And the guy helping her said something about an appraisal."

"Could be some insurance thing," Mollie said.

"Could be," Paul replied as he dried his hands. Returning to the bedroom he asked, "So, are you almost ready for a night out on the town?"

She giggled. "You're so corny."

He walked over, pulled her to him and said, "Yup, but I'm all yours."

She giggled again, kissed him and said, "I just need a few minutes."

CHAPTER 7

For the next three weeks Paige threw herself into her work. It was finally getting warmer outside but Paige locked herself in her office. She spent all of her time alone other than the occasional conversation with Gert who periodically brought her coffee as she worked around the clock on the breast cancer gala, determined to make it a rousing success. Chloe spent all of her free time with Chris, planning their cross-country adventure which would commence the day after the benefit. Spencer, purportedly still swamped at work, was also rarely home. With her life in limbo Paige found herself grateful for the isolation.

Gwen had cancelled their last two squash games, giving Paige an excuse to skip the gym or anything in public all together. Today she had promised Gwen and Mollie they would resume their ritual. However, as they all dressed in the locker room after working out Gwen received a text message and then announced, "Apologies ladies but I can't make brunch today. Something has come up."

"Is everything Ok?" Paige asked.

"Oh yes, yes. Just have to run. I'll make it up to you," she said, grabbing her bag and dashing out.

"Well, I guess it's just us," Mollie said.

"You know I'm actually thinking I may just head home if you don't mind."

"Oh, of course not, I, I just," Mollie stammered.

"Oh please don't misunderstand," Paige said, seeing Mollie's reaction. "I'm really not feeling very well but I didn't want to cancel my game with Gwen. Can we do it next week?"

"Of course," Mollie replied.

Trying to show Mollie she didn't mean to hurt her feelings Paige asked, "Are you ready? We can walk out together."

Mollie nodded and picked up her bag.

As they walked out and headed down the block Mollie asked, "So is Chloe getting excited for her big trip?"

"Yeah," Paige said wistfully. "I think so."

"You'll miss her, right? Is that it? I understand. When Tom and Jack left I didn't know what to do with myself. I had put all of my energy into them and then suddenly, poof, they're gone and the house is quiet and what to do."

Paige smiled and thought, *God, I'll miss her. I hadn't even realized how much I'll miss her.* Just then they were passing by the pottery place and Mollie said, "You know what, I think I'm going to drop in and check it out."

Paige stopped and looked at the sign. "Well, have a great time."

"Would you like to join me, if you're up to it?" Mollie asked.

"Oh I, I…"

"That's all right. Maybe another time," Mollie said.

Suddenly picturing the vast emptiness that awaited her at home Paige reconsidered. "You know, I would like to come in for a bit if you don't mind bringing a novice."

Mollie smiled excitedly and the two walked in.

Fifteen minutes later Paige, wearing a stained loaner smock, was being shown how to shape clay on a wheel. Her hands were covered with the rust colored substance as Mollie encouraged her, saying, "You'll get the hang of it. Just have fun."

As Paige pushed her fingers into the clay it was as if she was in conversation with all of the pieces of her life. With each press she was somehow trying to work them out or mold them together and make them stick; her mother, Jake, Chloe and most of all, Spencer.

Two hours later, standing outside, Mollie asked, "Do you think you'll give it another go sometime?"

"Maybe. I don't know. I was glad to finally try it."

"Well, I'm glad you had fun and that you're feeling better."

Paige smiled and said, "See you next week. Oh, and please don't forget to mark the breast cancer event in your calendar. I'm putting you and Paul on the list."

Mollie smiled, and Paige leaned in to hug her.

"Bye."

"Bye."

On the walk home Paige thought about how silly it was that her mother never let her take pottery classes. As it was, although the experience was cathartic, it hadn't lived up to her imagination. She wished she had figured that out years ago. It was then that she was confronted with a deeper realization: *You can never go back, you can only go forward.* By the time she arrived at home she was determined to speak to Spencer. The silence had gone on long enough and it was up to her to unlock it. As she walked in the front door, Gert came running to her. "What is it Gert? What's wrong?"

"I don't know. Chloe has locked herself in her room and I can hear her crying. I don't know what happened but she came home crying and ran straight into her room."

Paige handed her bag to Gert and hurried to Chloe's room. She knocked on the door and said, "Honey, it's me. Please open the door right now, I'm worried about you."

Chloe opened the door and Paige saw she had been crying for ages. Her mascara was streaked down her cheeks and her eyes were red and puffy. "Oh, Honey," Paige said, embracing her. "What is it? What's happened?"

"Chris and I broke up. It's over," she said before bursting into tears. Sobbing on Paige's chest she continued, "Our trip is off. Please don't make me go to Stanford. I just want to stay here."

Paige held her tightly, and closed her eyes.

*

Still unwilling to leave her room at dinner time, Paige went to the kitchen and instructed Gert to bring Chloe a tray to her room.

"Please tell her that she has to nibble at least a little, even if she doesn't feel like it. She is not to stop eating. I won't let her slide further down the rabbit hole."

"Yes, I will make sure she has something," Gert reassured her.

"Thank you. I'm going to wait for Spencer."

Paige started to walk away and then stopped, turned and added, "Gert, when Spencer comes home please give us a few minutes before serving dinner."

Gert nodded and Paige went to the dining room.

As she sat at the end of the table waiting for Spencer she thought about Chloe. At once she felt some relief that Chloe might not leave which would buy her more time, but she also felt enormous guilt. She had never seen Chloe so distraught. Seeing Chloe so tormented, as she had been over Jake, showed Paige how young she really had been. The more she thought about it the more it reminded her of when she and Jake broke up, and later when she learned about Kay-Kay. She started to question how it was that her own parents didn't even notice how devastated she was. Soon she was entranced wondering about it all. *Did they know about Jake? Were they waiting for it to end? Were they relieved? How did I get through that heartbreak alone? Is this the way of young love? Is it destined to end dramatically? Will Chloe learn to let it go or will it haunt her and shape her future relationships?* Paige was so engrossed wondering about Chloe and Chris that she lost track of time. A sudden slamming of the front door startled her, and she jumped up in her seat. Before she could call out to see what was going on, Spencer was urgently hollering, "Paige! Paige where are you?"

"I'm in here," she answered as she stood up.

Spencer hurried into the room and Paige said, "Did Gert call you? Do you know what's going on? You seem so frantic."

He shook his head and said, "I have to tell you something important."

Paige looked at him and he continued, "Redmond is in trouble." He took a breath and then, more slowly said, "He's in real trouble."

Totally caught off guard she sat back down and asked, "What do you mean? What kind of trouble?"

He loosened his tie and sat down in the chair kitty-corner to her. "The company is in ruins, it's totally collapsing. They owe more than they have. They're going to lose everything."

She gasped. "What do you mean they're going to lose everything? Surely they have other assets," she rebutted in disbelief.

Spencer shook his head. "He's liquidated everything. He's been pouring money in, trying to plug up the holes but there was nothing he could do. In another time we could have gotten it back on course or at least kept it quiet, but not these days."

"But," Paige said, trying to make sense of it.

"When he was scrambling to fix things he made some mistakes. Paige, there are some legal issues regarding mismanagement of funds," he said, now putting his hand on hers. "No one's going to end up in jail or anything but when he walks away it *will* be with nothing."

"I just can't believe it. Gwen never said a word."

"They were hoping to find a way out. That's why I've been working such long hours. I've been trying to help but at this point it's clear that there's nothing anyone can do."

"What?" she asked so softly it was nearly a whisper. "All this time you've been, you've been helping Redmond?" she asked, trying to process all of this. "But I thought, I assumed..."

"What? What did you think?" he asked.

"I, uh... it can wait. First tell me more. What can we do to help Redmond and Gwen? And if this has been going on for weeks or months, why are you telling me now? Is there something else?"

"The story is going to break and it's going to be bad. It's going to be on the front page Monday morning. Investors will lose money, people will lose their jobs. It's going to be terrible."

"Oh my god. I just can't believe it. How's Redmond handling this?"

"He's very depressed. I've been extremely worried about him. When he still thought there might be a way out he seemed to have some fight in him but since things have become clearer he's deteriorated."

"And Gwen? What about Gwen?"

"Two weeks ago he made a passing remark about how he had let her down, but that's all he's said and I didn't want to pry. I thought maybe she had said something to you."

Paige shook her head. "No, not a word. Although I guess she has been a bit strange lately, cancelling our plans a couple of times, but I've been so preoccupied I suppose I didn't pay attention."

Just then Gert came in. "I'm sorry to interrupt. Would you like me to serve dinner now?"

"Sure Gert. Thank you," Paige replied.

"I'm going to wash up. I'll be right back," Spencer said.

When Gert returned with the dinner plates Paige asked her to put Spencer's setting down next to her, where he had been sitting. "No need to sit on opposite sides, right?" she said as if to justify this change from the routine.

Gert smiled and did as she was asked.

A few minutes later they started eating a simple dinner of roast chicken, carrots and parsnips. After a few bites Spencer said, "You should call Gwen before the news hits."

Paige leaned her fork against the edge of her plate. "But what would I say? She obviously doesn't want anyone to know."

"Well everyone is going to know. Don't you think it's better to reach out before you've read about it in the *Wall Street Journal*?

"You know Gwen, she would be embarrassed."

They were silent for a moment, and Spencer took a long breath and looked at Paige. "Sometimes we need to put things out in the open, even when it's awful. Haven't you always believed that?"

Paige opened her mouth to respond but Spencer stopped her by saying, "Being embarrassed isn't the worst thing. People get over their pride and focus on what matters, eventually."

"She chose not to tell me so maybe I should respect her wishes and go along with it."

"Well her vanity is going to take a blow whether she can handle it or not."

"It's not vanity. I know that's the impression she gives but it isn't that at all. She likes to focus on the positive and make other people feel good."

"Paige, you need to call her."

She inhaled and agreed, "I know. Of course I'll reach out to her. I just don't know what to say."

He put his fork down and touched her hand for the second time that night. "You'll think of something," he said sweetly.

She smiled, and they returned their attention to dinner for a few minutes before Spencer said, "When I got home you said something about Gert calling to tell me something. What were you talking about?"

"I guess you could say it's been an eventful day. Chloe and Chris broke up. I don't know all of the details but Chloe has been locked in her room hysterical all day."

Spencer's eyes opened widely. "Wow. I didn't see that coming."

*

The next morning after her shower Paige decided to check on Chloe. She crept up to her room and pressed her ear against the door. Gert was passing by and smiled. Paige walked over to her and asked, "Do you know if she's still asleep?"

"I expect so. Poor thing, I heard her whimpering into the wee hours."

"Well, I don't want to disturb her. Can you please see that she eats something when she gets up? And thank you for staying last night."

"Of course."

"I think I'll go to my office and try to get some work done but please let me know if she gets up."

"Certainly."

"Thank you, Gert."

As Paige sat down at her desk, trying to focus, her thoughts drifted from Chloe to Gwen. *I need to try to reach her*, she thought. She left messages at Gwen's home and on her cell, asking for a return call. Afraid Gwen was avoiding her, she also sent her a text message that read:

LET'S MEET FOR COFFEE. HOW ABOUT THAT HOLE IN THE WALL W/THE OLD FASHIONED MARBLE CAKE?

In limbo waiting for Chloe to start stirring or to hear back from Gwen, she turned her computer on in the hopes of distracting herself with work. Just before she could open the gala folder, the telephone rang. She saw on the caller ID that it was Mollie.

"Hello."

"Oh, hi Paige. It's Mollie."

"Hi, Mollie. How are you?"

"Oh, I'm fine thanks. I know it's last minute and you're probably busy but Paul is watching some game today and I thought I might go to The MET. There's an impressionist exhibit I thought you might like to see."

Before Paige could respond Mollie said, "If you're busy with your family…"

"No, actually I was just, well I was just, doing nothing really. I'd love to join you. Shall we meet at the main entrance in half an hour?"

"That's great," Mollie said.

"See you then.

On the way out Paige stopped to see Gert. "I think I'll go out for a bit but please call me if Chloe needs me. Even if you're not sure, just call."

Gert smiled. "Yes, of course."

*

"Well, that was really amazing," Mollie said as they made their way out of the crowded exhibit.

"Quite a collection," Paige replied.

"I've always wanted to see Renoir's dancing couples in person. That was a treat."

"I saw two of them at the D'Orsay in Paris years ago but I've never seen all three together. I don't think I appreciated what he had captured. The contrast, seeing them side by side. It's provocative," Paige said.

"Yes, although I was surprised seeing them in person how similar they also are, except for the clothes," Mollie said with a giggle.

Paige smiled, and Mollie continued, "I also love seeing Monet's work. You know Paul and I have always wanted to visit his home in Giverny. Have you been there?"

Suddenly Paige stopped in her tracks.

"Paige? What is it?" Mollie asked, standing beside her.

"This painting," Paige said, transfixed on the painting hanging in front of them.

Mollie looked over and said, "Oh, that's..."

"It's *Seated Woman with a Parasol*," Paige interjected.

Mollie smiled and looked intently at the painting, mirroring Paige. "It's lovely," she said. "Paul and I saw it a few years ago in Chicago. It must be on loan."

Paige nodded, still staring at the painting. "When I was a girl I saw this in Chicago and my mother told me it was her favorite painting."

"Oh, that's nice," Mollie said. "Must bring back memories."

"I told my mother it reminded me of her, because the woman is dignified and disciplined. But looking at it now, I'm not sure I had it right."

"What do you see now?" Mollie asked.

"An illusion. That the appearance the woman is giving off isn't quite what it seems." She paused before lowering her voice and continuing, "The control is a facade. I used to think the woman was sitting so tall and now I think it looks more like someone put her there, put her there to sit like that."

"You know there's a song about this painting, I think by Tori Amos. Did you ever hear it?"

Paige shook her head and turned from the painting to Mollie. "How does it go?"

"Oh, I think it's something like, 'If I'm the seated woman with the parasol, I will be safe in my frame.' I think it's a song about betrayal."

Paige smiled, nodded slightly and returned her gaze to the painting. She whispered the words, "safe in my frame" and smiled again before saying, "Shall we head out? I'd like to get home to see Chloe."

Mollie agreed and the two made their way towards the exit. As they approached the door Paige heard her phone beep. She pulled it out of her bag and read a text from Gwen:

THAT SPENCER IS SUCH A RAT. I CAN BE THERE IN 20. THANK YOU.

Paige texted back:

ON MY WAY.

"Mollie, I hope you don't mind but I have to run. This was really lovely. Thank you for getting me here."

With that Paige leaned in and hugged Mollie tightly.

"Bye," she said warmly.

"Bye, Paige," Mollie said with a wave.

*

When Paige walked into the diner, lined with small booths on the left and a long counter with stools to the right, she immediately saw Gwen sitting in the far corner booth. As always, Gwen was impossible to miss, sporting oversized black sunglasses, a black trench coat and fire engine red lipstick. Paige headed straight to the back and slid into the booth opposite Gwen. Never one to give up on a grand entrance Gwen took off her glasses and dramatically tussled her hair before saying, "Oh darling, please don't look at me like I'm Marilyn in the sad days."

Paige smiled slightly, extended one of her arms across the table and placed her hand on Gwen's.

They sat for a moment before the waitress came over and asked, "What'll you have?"

Paige withdrew her hand and said, "Two coffees please, and a piece of marble cake to share."

After the waitress walked away Gwen said, "I didn't tell you because we were hoping…"

"I know." Paige hard-blinked her eyes, shook her head and said, "None of that matters one bit. Now tell me, how are you, really? How can I help?"

Gwen shrugged, "I'm trying to be upbeat for Redmond. He needs me to stay positive."

"Spencer said he seems depressed. You must be so worried."

"He sits in his chair in his study just staring at the walls. And he's been going out a lot and doesn't say where he's going but I know."

"Oh Gwen, do you think he's seeing someone?"

Just then the waitress came back and set down a piece of cake with two forks. She flipped over their coffee cups and filled them from a pot that looked like it was coated with tar. It seemed to take forever. "There's creamer and sugar and that packet stuff for you ladies on the table," she said.

"Thank you," Paige responded before returning her attention to Gwen.

"Maybe it's not a relationship, per se. You know there are escort services all over the city that wealthy men use to feel better about themselves. Maybe Redmond is..." but Gwen cut her off. "He's going to AA meetings. He's an alcoholic. Well, a recovering alcoholic."

Stunned, Paige asked, "Why didn't you ever say anything?"

"He hasn't had a drink in ages and he doesn't like people to know. He doesn't want to show weakness. You know how powerful men are."

"Are you concerned he may be drinking?" Paige asked.

"No, but I'm terrified that he wants to."

Gwen took a sip of her coffee before continuing, "I just can't believe this is happening to us."

"You'll get through this. Soon this will be a blip on the radar, that's all. You know Spencer and I will do anything we can to help. With Redmond's connections, he'll land on his feet."

Gwen nodded. "Spencer has been wonderful. I don't think Redmond would have kept it together this long without him."

They sat for a moment before Paige picked up a fork, cleaned it on her napkin and said, "Come on, let's try this thing,"

Gwen sighed, picked up her fork and took a nibble.

"So, are you ever going to tell me what it is about this cake?" Paige asked.

"My mother was a waitress at a 24-hour diner. I mean a real fries and gravy, trucker diner. She had terrible hours and sometimes, when she couldn't leave me at a neighbor's or my grandmother's she brought me to work with her and I slept in a booth. If I was quiet and stayed out of the way in the morning she would sneak me a piece of marble cake and a glass of milk. It had think fudge icing and... the sweetness seemed to cover up everything else about that experience."

Paige smiled. "You'll be Ok Gwen. You and Redmond will be Ok."

"I know."

*

Paige headed home with greater clarity than she had possessed in ages. When she arrived she marched straight to Chloe's room and knocked on the door. "Honey, it's me. Please open the door."

"She isn't home," Gert said from down the hall.

"Oh," Paige said, surprised. She walked towards Gert and asked, "Where did she go?"

"She said to tell you that she was going to a friend's and not to worry about her."

"Oh. I wanted to talk with her. Is Spencer home?"

"No."

"Ok, well I suppose I'll go to my office and get some work done but will you please let me know when either of them comes home?"

"Certainly. Can I bring you anything?"

"Some coffee would be wonderful, thank you."

Moments later Paige sat down at her computer, turned it on and opened her breast cancer gala folder. She couldn't stop thinking about Chloe and Spencer, wanting only to talk with them each and help make things better. Then she started thinking about Gwen, where she had come from and where she was going. She suddenly realized that what attracted her to Gwen was what had drawn her to Kay-Kay. They both had a brash honesty and full-throttle zest for life that she envied.

Before she knew it she was online googling Kayla Washington. She scanned the search results and clicked on the seventh one, a website for a dress shop in Brooklyn called *Designs by Kayla*. She clicked on the link for "formal wear" and then one by one she looked at the one-of-a-kind dresses that bore Kay-Kay's unmistakable fingerprint. In the section labeled "couture" there were stunning full-length gowns with hand done bead-work in all of the bold colors Kay-Kay loved. She began to wonder if any of them came from the sketches on Kay-Kay's bedroom wall where they had spent so many days studying and laughing. As she immersed herself into Kay-Kay's work she got an idea. Just then Gert knocked on the door to deliver Paige's coffee.

"Can I get you anything else?"

"No thank you. I'm going to be making some phone calls, but please do let me know if Chloe or Spencer return."

"Certainly," Gert said before closing the door behind her.

Paige took a deep breath and thought, *I'll deal with the past now, and the future later.* Then she went back into her gala folder and opened a document labeled VIP guests. The first name on the list was Diane Sawyer, who had long been a supporter and friend. She picked up the telephone and dialed her home number. "Hello, Diane. It's Paige Michaels. I'm calling to ask a favor."

Part Three

CHAPTER 8

At six o'clock Gert knocked on Paige's office door.

"Come in."

"I'm sorry to disturb you."

"It's fine. You're not disturbing me. Any word from Chloe or Spencer?"

"No, I'm afraid not," Gert replied before continuing, "It's getting a bit late and…"

"Oh forgive me Gert," Paige said, as she shook her head. "Of course you'd like to get home to your family. I'm so sorry for keeping you. I'm a bit preoccupied."

"It's no trouble at all. I wasn't sure about everyone's dinner plans so I left a roast cooling on the stove and a salad in the refrigerator."

"Thank you, Gert. Have a lovely evening."

After Gert shut the door, Paige retrieved her cellphone and sent Chloe a text:

WHERE ARE YOU? COMING HOME SOON?

Not a moment passed before Paige's phone beeped, indicating an incoming message which read:

SAMANTHA'S. MIND IF I STAY OVER?

Paige sighed and texted back:

FINE BUT I WANT TO TALK TO YOU TOMORROW. HOPE YOU'RE FEELING BETTER.

Chloe's return text simply said:

XO

Paige held her phone for a minute, savoring the last text before placing it back on her desk and muttering, "I hope she's Ok." Just then there was a loud knock on her door. Before she could say anything Spencer flung the door open and announced, "You won't believe it. There's a very slim chance – I mean a one in a million chance—we can put something together to pull Redmond and the lot of them out. I have to go to China with them. The jet is standing by. I just came home to tell you and grab a bag."

"Wow. Ah, I guess that's good news," she said, startled. "I'm not thrilled China always seems to be the answer, you know how I feel about their human rights issues. But I do so hope it works out for Gwen," she continued, starting to speak more softly. "When will you be back? I was hoping to talk with you."

"I'm not sure how long this will take. At least a few days I imagine."

"The situation with Chloe—she was supposed to leave for California next week and now she doesn't want to go at all."

"I know but the fact is that school doesn't start for months so if she cancels or postpones this road trip, is that really the worst thing? She can still start school in September. Do we really want our eighteen year old traipsing across the country? Honestly, I'm a bit relieved. Aren't you?"

"Now she's talking about not going to Stanford at all, and staying in New York. My own fear aside, I want her to do what will fulfill her, but I really don't know what's going on. And I'm concerned that she's so distressed. I was hoping to talk with her but she's at Samantha's tonight."

"I think it's a good sign that she went out. If there's reason to worry of course I'll come back, but this may be Redmond and Gwen's only shot at getting out of this mess. Don't you think I should try to help them?"

"Of course. I, I just…" but she didn't know quite what to say.

"I'll be back in a few days, a week at the most."

"My mother's benefit is next Saturday. You'll be back for it, won't you?"

"Yes. I've got to go and get some things together."

Paige nodded. "When you get back…"

Spencer tilted his head down and quietly said "Yes, I know." With that, he left the room.

*

As Mollie stood in the dressing room with fluorescent lights beating down on her head, she strained her neck to examine herself from every angle visible in the mirror. *I wonder if these are fat mirrors. I think they're distorted*, she thought to herself as she strained her neck in the other direction. *But why would they do that? It makes the clothes look bad, so they must not do that. It's more likely they'd have skinny mirrors so everything would look better. Oh god, if I look like this in skinny mirrors then...*

"Everything Ok in there?" the saleswoman called from the other side of the curtain, jarring Mollie back into the moment and causing her to wonder if her thoughts were so loud the woman actually heard them.

"Ah, yes. Thank you. Everything is fine."

"How are the alterations working out for you? If you need any adjustments I can call for the tailor."

"Um, I think it's Ok," Mollie said before turning around and sliding the curtain open.

"Oh, you look beautiful," the perky, size two saleswoman said. "That's a gorgeous color on you."

"Thanks," Mollie said, starting to feel better. "I've always loved royal blue."

"Come stand here," the saleswoman said, indicating a stand with three-way mirrors.

As Mollie stepped up and saw herself she smoothed the sides of her long gown, thinking how incredible the satin felt against her skin.

"It's just gorgeous," the saleswoman said. "I love the simple bodice, very flattering. I think it fits you well. How does it feel?"

"Oh, I think it feels good," Mollie said, again straining her neck to examine herself from every angle.

"Do you have shoes to wear with this? I'd be happy to bring you a few pairs to try on."

"Oh, I don't know. I have basic black pumps, and I also have a pale, blush colored pair that might work."

"You know those sound fine but if the event is very formal perhaps I could bring you something, just to see."

"Well it is a black tie event so maybe I should try something on. I'm a size 9. Do I need to go to the shoe department?"

The saleswoman inadvertently giggled. "I'll be happy to bring you a few selections, so you can try them on with the gown. I'll be right back."

"Oh, nothing too high. I'm not good with those pointy heels," Mollie called after her.

Not knowing what to do with herself Mollie went back into the dressing room and sat on the small ottoman, waiting. *She's been gone a long time. Maybe there's nothing in my size, my feet are too big. I hope the dress doesn't wrinkle. Maybe I should stand up,* but before she could the saleswoman called, "Mrs. Johnston?"

Mollie flung the curtain open to see the over-zealous saleswoman now standing with a stack of Jimmy Choo shoe boxes.

Mollie's heart started to beat a bit faster with anxiety over what she had gotten herself into. She had already spent a fortune on the gown, listening to Gwen's suggestion of going to Bergdorf's. *Oh no, if I sweat I'll mess up my dress, so I better calm down and try to relax.* The first pairs were sparkling strappy things that Mollie couldn't imagine wearing. *Oh my god, everyone will think I'm trying to look like some fashionable twenty-something.* Despite her instructions they all had high pointed heels that Mollie could barely walk in. Just before she was going to say she'd wear something she already had, and thereby relieve herself from the worry of over-spending, the saleswoman opened the last box.

"Now, I know these aren't the typical choice but I thought I should show you another way to go."

Mollie's jaw dropped. They were simple black satin slingbacks with a splattering of jewel colors—sapphire, emerald and ruby red—on the outward arch of each shoe. *If shoes are a canvass, these are Kandinsky meets Pollock,* she thought. They were the most beautiful shoes she had ever seen.

"I think the blue in the shoe will bring the look together," the saleswoman said, as Mollie slipped them on. "The heel is low too, so they may be more comfortable."

Mollie turned to look back in the mirror before emphatically saying, "I'll take them."

*

When Chloe got home she went straight to the kitchen and started scouring the refrigerator for something to eat.

"Chloe, Chloe is that you?" Paige called.

"I'm in the kitchen," Chloe hollered.

"What are you looking for?" Paige asked, suddenly behind her.

"Oh, gee," Chloe gasped. "You startled me," she said before closing the refrigerator.

"Sorry, Honey. Are you hungry? Can I get you something?"

"Yeah, I'm starving," Chloe said as she sat down at the table. "The food at Samantha's house is so gross. I barely ate anything."

"Glad to see you have an appetite. Gert made a roast. There are tons of leftovers, do you want some?"

"Ooh, gross, Mom. Don't we have any veggies or fruit or anything?"

"Um," she said, searching the refrigerator. "There are celery sticks. Do you want some with tuna or peanut butter or something?"

"Yeah, great," she said as she walked over to the pantry to get the peanut butter.

A moment later Paige set a small plate down with celery stalks, a small bottle of water, knife and a napkin and then she sat down.

"Thanks," Chloe said before opening the jar of peanut butter and sticking a piece of celery right into it.

"Oh, Chloe, use the knife."

"Sorry, Mom."

After Chloe took a couple of bites Paige asked, "Did you have a good time at Samantha's?"

Chloe shrugged.

"Have you talked to Chris?"

She shook her head.

"Chloe, what happened?"

"I don't want to talk about it."

"Was Chris with another girl?"

"God Mom, no, but I said I don't want to talk about it."

Paige sighed. "Well then let's talk about Stanford."

"Mom, I don't want to talk about it," she said, exasperated.

"Look, I can see you're upset and if you don't want to talk about Chris I won't push you but we need to talk about school. You can't just declare you're not going, and that's it."

"I thought you'd be happy if I stay. It hasn't seemed like you wanted me to go."

Paige's heart sank. "I'm sorry if it seemed that way. I should have been more excited for you. I guess I also thought I'd be happier if you stayed, and the selfish part of me still does but…"

"But what?"

"But I know this isn't really what you want. You always wanted to go to California, long before Chris. I think you'll regret giving up this opportunity to go somewhere new and forge your own path. And if you and Chris are really over then you shouldn't be making major life choices just as a reaction to the split."

Chloe thought for a minute before saying, "And what if we're not really over? Mom, I might have made a huge mistake. I don't know, I think I got scared and…"

"Then fix it, or, at least try to fix it."

"Do you really think Chris and I are even meant to be?"

Paige smiled and said, "Honestly, probably not. Chloe you are sooo young. I know you may not feel that way now, but you are. You can't yet even imagine who you will become. I think you have many great loves ahead of you. But I also know that if you walk away impulsively and end something prematurely you may live to regret it. First love is very special, whether it's meant to last or not, and I think you should see it through. And even if you can't work it out with Chris, or you decide you don't want to, end it the right way. If you do that, there's nothing stopping you from going to Stanford as you planned regardless of Chris. You can spend the summer here if you don't road trip."

"I'll think about it, Ok?"

Paige lowered her eyelids in agreement. "I'm here if you need me. Please talk to me, if you want to."

She nodded, got up and gave Paige a kiss on the top of her head. Chloe started to walk away when Paige noticed her dirty dishes left behind. Paige rolled her eyes and called after her, "Uh excuse me. Please clean up after yourself."

*

The next few days lingered. Chloe seemed to always be out. Paige didn't ask questions, not wanting to pressure her. Spencer emailed a couple of times to say that it was slow-going and that he didn't know when he'd be back. His emails were curt and there was no signature line at all to indicate how he felt about her, or even that he intended to be friendly. Paige started to imagine the worst—that whatever progress they had made evaporated like the trail of jet fuel between them. Every time she started to entertain these destructive thoughts she heard her mother's voice saying *stay on course, don't lose sight of the big picture*, and she was able to resume her work.

The more immersed she became in the final details of the breast cancer event, the more frequently she found herself thinking about her mother. She couldn't imagine the strength it took for Eleanor to keep so much in and the terrible toll it must have taken. She suspected that the distance she always felt with her mother was because Eleanor had learned to withhold and keep self-contained. It was her survival strategy. Paige understood. But if these past months had taught her anything, it was the terrible burden of trying to live in silence. This realization caused her to wonder about her relationship with her own daughter. Paige hoped she had taught Chloe to embrace love and life and to make her way in the world, but she feared that when she got off track Chloe may have too, and she wasn't available to catch it in time. Between thoughts of Chloe, Eleanor and her work, Paige was startled when Gert knocked on her office door.

"Uh, yes. Come in."

"Sorry to disturb you. I just came to remove your lunch tray."

"Oh, yes. Thank you, Gert."

Gert took the tray from Paige's desk and started to walk away before turning to ask, "If it will be just you for dinner tonight shall I make you the roasted tilapia you like?"

"You're so thoughtful. That would be nice. Thank you."

As Gert started to leave the room Paige called after her. "On second thought, you don't need to make anything for me."

Gert nodded and left the room, shutting the door behind her. Paige picked up her cellphone and sent Chloe a text:

CHLOE, DON'T PUT YOURSELF IN A FRAME. LEAP OFF THE CANVASS AND INTO YOUR LIFE.

A moment later her phone beeped and she read Chloe's response:

HUH? WHAT ARE YOU ON? CAN I HAVE SOME?

Paige giggled and responded:

LEAP INTO YOUR LIFE, SWEET GIRL.

Chloe responded:

XOXO

Paige smiled and then texted Gwen:

WHY ARE WE BOTH ALONE WHEN WE COULD BE TOGETHER? COME OVER FOR DINNER. WE CAN ORDER CHINESE IN HONOR OF REDMOND AND SPENCER.

Gwen instantly replied:

I'LL BRING THE VODKA.

Paige laughed and responded:

SPLENDID. SEE YOU AT 7.

Gwen texted back:

INVITE MOLLIE SO IT WON'T BE DEPRESSING.

Paige laughed again and responded:

WILL DO

*

As soon as Mollie hung up with Paige, she tried to call Paul at the office. She was so excited that she misdialed and had to try a second time before getting through.

"Paul Johnston's office. May I help you?"

"Hi, Helen. It's Mollie. Is Paul free?"

"Sure, Mollie. Please hold."

As she waited for Paul to pick up she suddenly realized how rude she was to Helen. She normally asked how she was but in her exhilaration it slipped her mind.

"Hi, Honey."

"Oh, hi, Hon. Do you have a minute?"

"For you? Always."

"Paige just called me out of the blue and asked if I wanted to go to her house for dinner tonight. I guess Spencer and Redmond are out of town or something and she thought we could do a gal's night with Gwen. I've never seen her home before. I bet it's amazing."

"Sounds like fun."

"I could fix you something for dinner so you could just heat it up."

"I can pick up a sandwich on the way home to save you the trouble. It's an opportunity to try that new deli."

"Thanks. I'm sure I won't be home late."

"Have a good time."

"Ok, great. Thanks."

"I love you."

"Love you too."

"Bye."

"Bye."

After hanging up the phone, Mollie went directly to her bedroom closet to figure out what to wear. She started sifting through her tops but nothing seemed quite right. She took several tops out along with a few pairs of pants and threw them all over her bed. *Oh, that won't work. I can't wear stretch pants. If I wear the silk blouse they may think I'm too dressy. It's just a night in, I should be casual* she thought as she picked up a sweater and paired it with black cotton pants. *But if I'm too casual I won't be comfortable.* She continued to mix and match the clothes strewn all over her bed. Eventually she thought, *I'm just being silly,* and she grabbed her favorite jeans and light blue knit sweater. *I should go and pick up a bottle of wine to bring. But how would I know what to get, they're probably connoisseurs. Oooh, instead I could bring a special dessert. But they don't eat sweets. I wonder if you can bring a dessert when you know the hostess doesn't eat dessert, although Paige did try that stickybun so maybe… I wonder what the etiquette is in this kind of situation.*

She thought back to the many dinner parties she used to host in New Jersey and decided the most common hostess gifts were flowers, wine or dessert although some people brought a coffee table book. After a little more back and forth she decided there was plenty of time to go to her favorite pastry shop in Little Italy to get something special. They boasted the best cannoli and creampuffs in the city and Mollie thought the mini size would be perfect. *It is the thought that counts anyway and this is thoughtful. Besides I have the time to kill so I might as well make the effort. Plus if they just serve salad or teeny-tiny food at least I'll have something to eat.*

Three hours later Mollie was hailing a cab while trying to hold the small hot pink pastry box flat in one hand and the flowers and white wine she couldn't help herself from getting in the other. She was thrilled when a taxi finally pulled over. As she got into the car she asked the driver to please wait while she buckled up and carefully positioned the box on her lap.

Mollie looked out the window the entire way to Paige's, taking in all there was to see. Every time the cabbie stopped short or hit a pothole Mollie held tightly onto the pastry box, praying nothing was smooshed. Soon she was there. Flustered when the doorman opened the car door, Mollie held out the wine and flowers in one hand prompting him to say, "I'll take those for you, while you get out." She smiled nervously, clinging to the box in her other hand. With the driver paid and in possession of all of her items, she walked into the lobby where she slowed her pace to admire the impressive crystal chandelier. The doorman asked where she was heading. "Oh, to Paige Michaels. My name is Mollie…" but before she could finish he said, "Yes, Mrs. Johnston. You're expected. Right this way," and he led her to the Michael's elevator. As she travelled up she tried not to fidget, although it was hard holding so many things in just the right position. A moment passed, and a chime sounded before the elevator door opened. She had arrived.

*

"Oh, let me help you," Paige said as she took the pastry box from Mollie, before either could say hello. "Come in, please," she said.

Mollie walked in and exclaimed, "Your home is stunning."

"Thank you. We've always loved it here. Please, come and put your things down."

As they walked from the foyer to the kitchen, Paige asked, "So dare I ask what is in this little package?"

"I went to a bakery in Little Italy and picked up some bite size treats for dessert."

"Wonderful. Thank you."

Mollie smiled.

"And since they're bite size we may even convince Gwen to splurge."

Mollie laughed. "Is she here?"

"I suspect she will be making her entrance any minute now. Here, why don't you give me those," Paige said, gesturing to the flowers and wine. "How lovely," she said as she smelled the bouquet. "White flowers are my favorite."

"Yes, I remember you mentioned that," Mollie said as she placed her handbag on a chair.

"You're so thoughtful, Mollie, really," Paige said as she opened cabinets in search of a vase.

"I just have a good memory."

"Uh, yes, you always did," Paige replied, still searching the cabinets. "I'm not as incompetent as I seem but our housekeeper usually does this and I'm afraid she's moved some things around. Ah, there we go," she said as she removed a simple crystal vase.

"You didn't have to bring so much," she said as she put the flowers in water.

"Oh, I…" but they were interrupted by the doorbell.

"That must be Gwen, and barely late at all. I'll go get her. Please, make yourself comfortable."

Mollie sat down at a stool by the counter and looked around the room. It was as if she had stepped into *Home and Garden* magazine, where everything is so perfect you can't believe anyone lives there. She had never seen such an immaculate kitchen and wondered how they kept the white so clean. There were little touches everywhere, a green bud vase with a white rose, white hand towels with yellow trim neatly hanging on a rack and a large white bowl filled with limes and lemons. She was lost in thought when Paige and Gwen came into the room.

Gwen was wearing skinny dark blue jeans, high-heeled black leather boots and a large black shawl draped around her. Mollie suspected this was as casual as Gwen gets, but she still looked like she could walk a red carpet. Mollie started to get up and Gwen said, "Oh no darling, don't get up," as she walked over, squeezed Mollie's shoulder and gave her an air kiss.

"How are you?" Mollie asked.

She held up a bottle of vodka and said, "I'm exhausted. Let's talk about you darling."

"Let me take that," Paige said as she took the bottle from Gwen. "I'll stick it in the freezer for later. Mollie brought a lovely bottle of Pinot Grigio. Perfect with Chinese. Why don't we start with this?" she said as she picked up the bottle from the counter.

Mollie was thrilled to learn she had chosen well.

Gwen smiled. "Fabulous."

"I pre-ordered dinner earlier and it should be here in about fifteen minutes. Why don't you two go sit in the dining room. I'll open the wine and join you in a moment."

"Have you seen the house?" Gwen asked Mollie.

"Uh, no. I haven't."

"Well why don't I give Mollie a little tour and we'll meet you in the living room?" Gwen asked in a way that made clear she was not waiting for a response.

"Come, Mollie," Gwen said as she threw her shawl and handbag on a kitchen chair and headed out of the room.

"Please, feel free to look around," Paige said. "I should have offered myself."

Mollie smiled and jumped off her stool, hurrying to catch up to Gwen.

Displaying her background in high-end Manhattan real estate, Gwen shared some of the history of the area and pointed out various architectural elements in the penthouse. As Gwen spoke, Mollie thought about how impeccable Paige's taste was. Every detail was absolutely perfect. Soon they heard the doorbell ring and realized they had taken longer than intended.

"Oh dear, I hope Paige hasn't been bored waiting for us."

Gwen shook her head. "Nonsense."

Mollie started to make her way to the dining room, with Gwen following behind.

The table was beautifully set with simple bone white china, crystal glasses and linen napkins. Mollie was overjoyed to see her flowers as the centerpiece. Gwen sat down as Paige called from the kitchen, "I'm just putting the food in serving dishes. Help yourself to some wine."

Gwen started to pour herself a glass of wine.

Mollie, still standing in front of her chair called, "Can I help you?"

"I'm fine, thank you."

With that Paige came into the room holding two bowls which she placed on the table. "Please, sit down and pour some wine, Mollie. I'll be back in a moment."

Mollie sat opposite Gwen, leaving the seat at the head of the table open. Paige returned with two large plates, which she also placed on the table.

Mollie surveyed the food, which appeared to be steamed vegetables, steamed fish with ginger, sautéed pea pods and some suspiciously plain looking chicken skewers. And there wasn't any rice in sight. *I've never seen Chinese food served without rice,* Mollie thought.

"Everything looks wonderful," Gwen said as she picked up sterling silver tongs and began placing vegetables and chicken on her plate.

"Oh, yes, thank you so much for getting dinner, Paige," Mollie said.

"I hope you don't mind that I took the liberty of ordering for us. With the gala days away I know we all need to watch our waistlines. This place is wonderful—no MSG, no gluten, no sugar."

"No taste!" Gwen proclaimed, before breaking out into laughter.

Paige gave her a stern look and she said, "Oh I'm just joking darling. This is superb. Nothing worse for a girl's figure than salt. No detox can cure one of that bloat."

"It looks great, Paige," Mollie said as she started to take some food.

Paige and Gwen ate so little that there was plenty for Mollie, who helped herself to a second plate without thinking twice. To her surprise the food was delicious. The fish had deep, aromatic flavors, and was an unexpected pleasure.

During dinner they chatted about New York real estate, art exhibits of interest and the latest gossip about other members of the health club. When there was a lull in the conversation Mollie asked what brought Spencer and Redmond to China.

Paige opened her mouth to respond and Gwen jumped in with, "Oh some dreadfully boring meetings. Let's just hope they're not living it up too much at night. You know how it is there, how they try to impress American businessmen."

Mollie looked confused.

"You know, they bring them to those sex clubs where…."

Paige interrupted, "Now really Gwen, you're too much. They would never."

"Oh I know. I'm just teasing."

"The women that are traded between these men like commodities are some of the most exploited in the world. You can't imagine what their lives are like. Last year WIN did a…" before she could go on Gwen interrupted with a pronounced eye roll. "Yes, yes, it's terrible. I know." She then turned to Mollie and said, "One mustn't joke about whores with Paige."

Mollie had such a look of shock on her face that Gwen started laughing hysterically, followed immediately by Paige.

Mollie smiled and said, "Gosh you two are great."

"We've laughed our way through a lot of stuff," Gwen said.

Paige turned to Mollie and said, "Gwen has taught me the value of having a friend who isn't afraid to say anything."

Then Gwen, looking more serious than Mollie had ever seen her, said, "Paige is a wonderful friend because she understands restraint more than anyone I know, and she's smart enough to know its value, and you see, that is much a rarer gift."

Mollie smiled as Paige gently shook her head.

"And Mollie, I must say you are a welcome surprise," Gwen added.

Mollie was beaming but unsure of what to say. Before she could respond Paige said, "Yes, Gwen is right. I'm so glad to have reconnected with you and gotten to know you better."

"I feel the same way. And oh, I'm just so excited about the benefit. Will Spencer and Redmond make it back in time?

Paige nodded. "Yes."

"They wouldn't dare miss it," Gwen declared.

"Shall we have dessert in the living room?" Paige asked.

"Are you mad? I have to fit into Valentino in two days!" Gwen proclaimed. "Although is it even Valentino really now that that darling little man isn't at the helm of his own company?"

Paige rolled her eyes and continued, "Mollie brought some lovely pastries. I'll make some decaf and serve them in the living room."

"Well if you add some of that lovely vodka to the decaf, I'm in."

They all laughed and Paige agreed.

Before long they were sitting on the floor around the coffee table with their shoes off, a third of the way through the vodka, finishing the box of pastries and laughing so hard Mollie's face hurt.

When Mollie finally got home she found Paul half asleep watching television in bed. He woke up when she came in and she said, "Oh, I'm sorry you waited up for me."

"That's ok. What time is it?" he asked groggily.

"It's late. I'm sorry. We just got to talking and lost track of time," she said.

Paul yawned, picked up the remote to turn the television off and said, "Well, it sounds like you had a good time."

"Uh huh. It was great. Paige's place is spectacular and Gwen is hysterical."

"What did you have for dinner?"

"Nothing you would have wanted to eat. Paige ordered Chinese food but it was like no food you've ever seen before. It was all plain. There wasn't even rice."

"Well that's strange," he said, trying to show interest although clearly exhausted.

"Actually it was a lot better than it sounds, but you wouldn't have been happy."

Nodding off again, he mumbled "Uh huh."

Minutes later Mollie returned from the bathroom, turned the light off and slipped into bed, jarring Paul again. He scooted up behind her and put one of his arms around her. "Love you," he whispered as he drifted back to asleep.

CHAPTER 9

I don't remember the last time I slept so soundly, Paige thought as she opened her eyes and adjusted to the first morning light, looking at the empty space beside her. *I can't believe this day is here. This is really it. Today I need to do everything right. Tomorrow it all changes.*

It was the day of the benefit and Spencer's business had taken longer than anticipated but he had sent word that he would make it back in time for the big event. Paige heard Chloe come home late the night before so she decided to let her sleep in. *I wonder how she's doing. I bet she was with Chris. Maybe she'll want to talk. I hope she remembered to pick up her shoes. Stay on course Paige. One thing at a time. This will be a long couple of days. I'll need some energy, better make it a long run.*

After her run she stopped in the kitchen. "Good morning, Gert. I'm going to take a quick shower and then would you please bring breakfast to my office? I want to attend to some last minute details before the glam-team arrives."

"Certainly."

"Oh, did the tailor messenger over the gown?"

"Yes. It's hanging on your closet door."

"Thank you, Gert."

Twenty minutes later Gert delivered her breakfast. As Paige was pouring a cup of coffee there was a knock her door. "What did you forget, Gert?" she called.

"Oh, it's me Mom," Chloe said, standing in the doorway, still in her pajamas.

"Sorry, Honey. Come on in," she said.

Chloe floated into the room grinning like a Cheshire cat. She plopped down on the Victorian fainting couch, kicked her legs up and put her hands behind her head as she reclined. "Weeeeell, aren't you going to ask me?"

"Ask you what?" Paige said coyly.

"Oh, Mom," she said as she sat up straight.

"Let me guess, you and Chris, did you…"

127

"Yeah, we did," Chloe cut her off. "You were so right. I was making a huge mistake."

Paige smiled. "It's wonderful to see you so happy."

"Ooh, I better get moving. I hope Gert left me some coffee," Chloe said as she leapt up and started walking to the door.

"What's the rush? There's plenty of time."

"I haven't packed a thing."

"Packed for what?"

"For our trip. We leave tomorrow. Remember? That was the deal. I would stay until the benefit and leave the next day."

"Yes, of course I remember but I just assumed in light of everything you'd wait a bit. There's no reason to leave so quickly, is there?"

"I just don't want to waste a minute of what could be. You know? I'm in love. I'm in love and I'm going to see it through. Ok? But I don't have a thing packed and while Gert said she would send my things ahead to Stanford in August I still need to get enough together for the summer which is crazy when I only have today and…"

"Ok, I hear you," Paige said, interrupting the enthusiastic rant. "Of course you should follow your bliss. It's just, well, it won't be easy to see you leave."

Chloe walked over to Paige, leaned down and hugged her tightly. She kissed the top of her head and said, "I don't blame you, I would miss me too," before breaking out into laughter.

Paige laughed too and said, "Well you better get to it because the team will be here in a couple of hours and then you're all mine for the rest of the day."

Chloe rolled her eyes before conceding.

As she was leaving Paige called after, "Make sure your gown fits. And you have your shoes, right?"

Chloe nodded as she left the room, with her long, loose, perfect curls bobbing up and down as she walked away.

*

Mollie awoke to an empty bed and sweet smells swirling in the air. She put on her robe, brushed her teeth and walked into the main living space where she found Paul sitting at the table, reading the newspaper. "Good morning, beautiful," he said, folding the paper over to smile at her. "There's a fresh pot of coffee and a little treat waiting for you."

Curious, Mollie walked into the kitchen to discover a pastry box tied with white string. "Oh what did you do Paul?"

He laughed, "You'll see."

She snipped the string with a scissor, opened the lid and took in the aroma of sweet cinnamon, pecan sticky buns. Glaze was dripping off the top, revealing that they were still warm.

"What did you do, go when they opened?"

"Yup."

Mollie took two plates out of the cabinet and brought them to the table, along with the pastries. "Can I get you some coffee or did you already have yours?"

"I waited for you," he said.

As Mollie fixed two cups of coffee she called, "You really shouldn't have done this. I have to fit into my gown tonight."

"I can't imagine how today's breakfast will impact how you fit into your dress."

She handed Paul his coffee, sat down and served them each a stickybun.

Mollie took a bite, and while still chewing said, "I guess if I skip lunch today it'll be like I broke even. And thank goodness for shapers."

Paul furrowed his brow and said, "I have a better idea. I was thinking about a fun day out, just the two of us. But if you really don't want lunch you can just have popcorn."

"Popcorn?"

"There's a double-feature of those old Hitchcock movies, *Vertigo* and *Marnie*, which I think were two of his best. It would be great to see them on the big screen. This is one of those great things New York offers that we should take advantage of."

"Well I have to get ready for the benefit. I still need to get a manicure."

"The movies end around four o'clock. There are those walk-in nail places on every block. After the movies I can take you to get your nails done and you'll still have plenty of time to get all dolled up."

"What will you do while I'm getting my nails done?"

"I'll wait for you or I'll walk around a bit. Don't worry about me. What do you say?"

"Sure. Sounds great," she said before taking another big bite.

They left their apartment an hour later. With time to spare and wanting to soak up the gorgeous weather, Mollie and Paul took a long walk around the city, looking in store windows and chatting with the occasional street vendor. On crowded sidewalks Paul held Mollie's hand tightly, and when the crowds dissipated he walked with his arm around her waist. She saw an antique pocket watch in a shop window and stopped to show it to him, knowing he would appreciate it. When they arrived at the cinema and saw the long line Mollie panicked but Paul whipped two tickets out of his back pocket and said, "I ordered them online when you were in the shower."

He handed her a ticket and suggested, "Why don't you pick out some good seats and I'll get snacks."

Twenty minutes later they were sitting in a dark theatre, watching the opening scene of *Vertigo*, each with one hand in a large popcorn bucket Paul held between them.

When the movie ended the lights came on and there was an announcement that there would be a fifteen minute intermission before *Marnie*. Mollie jumped up, "I'm running to the ladies room before the line gets too long."

"I'm coming too, I want to stretch my legs," he said.

Despite her efforts to beat the crowd Mollie waited in a long line and made it back to the theatre as the lights were going down. She was surprised to have beaten Paul back. She turned her head to the back door, searching for Paul when she thought she saw Gwen sitting in the far corner of the theatre. Just then Paul sat down and handed her a bottled water. He leaned in and whispered, "I had a long wait."

As soon as *Marnie* ended and the house lights came on Mollie turned to where she thought she had seen Gwen, but the seat was empty. She scanned the room but there was no sign of her. Paul stood up and said, "Are you ready?"

"Uh huh," she said as she picked up her pocketbook and took his hand.

"I thought those were super. The scenery in *Vertigo* in particular was really done justice seeing it this way. He really was the master of suspense."

"Uh huh," she replied, distracted. "Oh, I'm sorry. I could have sworn I saw Gwen here," she said, still gazing around as they slowly made their way out of the theatre.

"Maybe it was just someone who looked like her. Now wouldn't that be ironic, in light of *Vertigo*?!" He broke out into hysterics and eventually Mollie laughed too.

"Ok, so now we better find you someplace to get your nails done."

Mollie nodded, turning her head one last time.

*

Knowing it might be the last time they got ready together, Paige savored her afternoon with Chloe. While getting their hair and makeup done in Paige's dressing room, they posed and made jokes about who had the best scary model looks, a game they had played for years to poke fun at the whole getting-glam process. They giggled their way through the afternoon wearing the matching terrycloth robes Spencer had given them for Valentine's Day the year before. Chloe went to her own room to put her dress on and returned to show it to Paige. She intended to show off, walking in and making a grand model pose, but instead her jaw dropped when she saw her mother. "Wow!" she exclaimed while shaking her head, in disbelief.

"Is it all right do you think?" Paige asked.

"Uh, it's amazing. You look amazing! I've just never seen you like, like…"

"Oh god, like what? Is it too much?"

"No Mom. It's just the right amount."

"Thanks, Honey," Paige said as she looked herself over in the large mirror.

Chloe sat on the edge of Paige's bed and said, "But I have to ask, are you having some kind of mid-life, uh mid-life…"

"Oh my god," Paige said as she turned in horror. "It looks like I'm having a midlife crisis?"

"No. No, that's not what I meant. It's just sooo different than what you normally wear. It's like you're not…"

"I'm not what?"

"You're not trying to blend in anymore. It's like you're not trying to fit a mold. Like you're over it, which is great really… But I have to ask, is this some weird way of giving Grandma the finger or something?"

"Heavens no!" Paige exclaimed. "This entire evening is intended to honor your grandmother. The dress, well, I have my reasons. You know this was my favorite color when I was a little girl. Anyway, it feels like the one for tonight but you have to tell me, is it all right?"

"You look radiant." Chloe paused before continuing, "What I said before wasn't what I meant. It's like you're letting everyone see the you that I know."

Paige smiled. "That's sweet. Well, now I know it's the right dress for tonight. Thank you."

"Ok, I really need to go and pick up Chris. Are you sure Jerry can drive us?"

"Yes, we got a limousine for the night. The red carpet at this event is important so…"

"Got ya. Well, you look awesome. Hope Dad makes it."

"Me too," Paige said longingly.

"See you there," Chloe said as she hopped off the bed and left.

Paige looked at herself one more time, wishing Spencer was there. She put her formal black trench coat on, picked up her sparkling clutch and decided she had no choice but to go without him. As she headed to the front door she heard it fly open, and Spencer hurry in, tossing his luggage on the floor. "I know how late I am and I'm sorry. We had trouble taking off and blah-blah. I can be ready in ten minutes."

"I can't miss the arrivals," she called after as he raced to the bedroom.

"Ten minutes," he shouted. "I won't let you miss it. I promise."

Spencer returned wearing his tuxedo and looking so handsome that Paige momentarily forgot how rushed they were and stood in the entranceway staring at him. *He is the sexiest man I have ever seen, after all these years. I'm so lucky. How could I have let it unravel?*

"Come on," he said gently as he grabbed her hand and they headed out the door.

On the way to the event Paige asked the limo driver to please take her coat once she was on the red carpet.

"Hmm, that's not like you, to make a big reveal," Spencer said. "Didn't you always say that the clothes shouldn't upstage the cause? What would Eleanor say?"

She rolled her eyes playfully. "Leave it to you to remember everything I've said. Actually, tonight I'm wearing something special and I planned to tell you about it beforehand but..."

He touched her hand and said, "I'm just teasing you. We only have a minute before we get there and I should prepare you that..."

"Oh no... It didn't go well?"

He shook his head. "It's over, there's nothing more to do. It will probably break on Monday or Tuesday at the latest."

"I was so hoping it would work out for them."

"Me too. And a lot of people will lose their jobs, their retirement funds, everything," Spencer replied as they pulled up. Paige watched as guests before them negotiated the red carpet, which was lined by a sea of onlookers and reporters, waiting to greet VIPs.

Their driver pulled over, opened the doors and they exited the car to a frenzy of camera flashes. Paige immediately noticed Diane Sawyer talking with a reporter and they smiled at each other. Side by side at the start of the red carpet, Paige handed Spencer her clutch while their driver removed her coat. There was an audible sigh of envy from the crowd as Paige showed off a body-hugging aqua gown, that opened slightly into a beautiful drape at the bottom. The sheer fabric was sprinkled with sparkles that glistened with each camera flash. Paige turned slightly to Spencer who was sporting the most impossibly boyish grin she had ever seen. "I can see why you wanted to make a big reveal," he said.

She smiled.

"You're breathtaking," he said. Before she could respond Giuliana Rancic from E-News made her way over and asked, "Mrs. Michaels, tonight will bring much needed attention and resources to breast cancer research which as you know is something that has personally affected me. Can you tell me what inspired you to host this event?"

"We lost my mother, Eleanor Michaels to breast cancer so naturally I feel compelled to do what I can to raise funds for research and to honor her legacy."

"Is there anything you would like to share with us about your mother?"

"My mother had a remarkable quiet elegance. She was dignity and grace personified."

"Before I let you go, I have to ask, because your gown is stunning. Who is it by?"

"Thank you. It's a Kayla Washington design."

"Well that must be at least the third I've heard that name tonight! I think it's safe to say there is a hot new designer on the scene. Thank you so much for stopping to chat with us and for all of your good work."

Paige nodded politely and thanked her. Then Spencer took her arm and they continued to make their way inside, talking with reporters along the way.

As they entered the enormous banquet hall, Paige surveyed the room, making certain everything was in place. Guests were ushered into a large open area used first for the cocktail hour and later, for dancing. A jazz trio played in the background. From a distance she saw the round dinner tables, draped in gold, and beyond the tables the stage where she would speak. Candle light bouncing off of the large crystal chandeliers and vases overflowing with white and blush flowers bathed the room in a champagne-colored glow. Even the parquet floor seemed to be shimmering.

The guests were sparkling too, with coutured women and tuxedo-clad men. Waiters in white coats walked around offering champagne, caviar toasts, artichoke hearts topped with mushroom duxelle and smoked salmon served in leaves of Belgian endive, a favorite of Eleanor's. The fundraising effort included a silent auction and so tables featuring donated items to bid on, including exotic trips, celebrity experiences, jewelry and high-end liquor lined the walls.

Paige and Spencer were consumed greeting friends and guests. When they finally had a minute to themselves Spencer whispered, "I think I should go bid on something, to set a tone."

Paige nodded and was barely alone for a moment before Mollie and Paul arrived. Paige smiled brightly as they came over and immediately leaned in to hug Mollie and then kiss Paul on the cheek.

"You look absolutely beautiful, Mollie."

"She sure does," Paul said, beaming as he looked at his wife.

Mollie blushed. "Thank you. And wow, you look incredible Paige. And you've made this magnificent room even more spectacular. Look at how the details in the crown molding are reflected in the flower arrangements, and the incredible gold leaf detailing is accentuated by the gold tablecloths" she said, looking all around.

"You have the best eye," Paige said.

"You've always had wonderful attention to detail, Paige," Mollie replied.

"Thank you both for coming. I'm so glad to have friends here."

"We're honored to be included. It's not every day you get to see someplace like this. Where's Spencer?" Paul asked.

"Oh, he's just over there," she said as she turned to point and noticed him making his way back to the group.

"Good to see you," Spencer said as he shook Paul's hand. "And Mollie, you look lovely. I was just bidding on a rare bottle of wine, so if I win we'll have to find a time to get together and drink it."

Paige looked at him curiously, and everyone smiled.

"Mollie, your shoes are fantastic, I just noticed them," Paige said.

"Thank you. They're new."

"They suit you well. And look how the colors are echoed in your exquisite opal ring. Is it an heirloom?"

"It was a gift from Paul. It's an antique," Mollie replied, beaming.

Over the next forty minutes Paige and Spencer continued to greet guests, introducing Mollie and Paul to everyone they spoke with. While celebrity never mattered to Paul, even he was a bit star struck chatting with Caroline Kennedy.

Just when Paige was wondering if Gwen and Redmond were going to come under the circumstances, Spencer gripped Paige's hand and made a nod towards the door. Everyone turned to look as Gwen and Redmond walked in, smiling and waving to people around the room.

"Unbelievable," Spencer muttered.

Paige squeezed his hand and subtly shook her head.

Gwen was wearing a strapless red gown, with an oversized bow on the back. It looked just like Marilyn Monroe's famous hot pink dress, but in Valentino red. With fire engine lips, a large diamond cuff bracelet and matching earrings, it was a show stopping looking.

Spencer leaned in and whispered, "How do you think it will look to people when she's photographed like that? They'll probably run the picture next to headlines about people losing their retirement funds."

Paige squeezed his hand again, and Paul said, "Boy, she sure knows how to make an entrance!"

Mollie gave him a sideways glance, and he stopped smiling.

As Gwen and Redmond reached the group Paige said, "You look beautiful, Gwen."

"Well thank you darling but I think the more pressing compliment must go to you. I never thought I'd see the day. Holy shit, you are smoking hot!"

"I think what she means to say is, you look lovely Paige," Redmond said as he leaned in to kiss Paige on the cheek.

"I meant to say she looks damn hot," Gwen said playfully. "Don't you think Spencer?"

Noticing Paige blink nervously, Gwen shifted the attention off of Spencer and Paige by exuberantly acknowledging Mollie and Paul.

"You know I think the opening remarks are going to begin any moment. Perhaps we should go to our table," Paige said.

"Oh, Paul and I didn't have a chance to go to get our seat assignments yet, we need to go over to the place card table first" Mollie responded.

"No need. You're at our table. It's the six of us and Chloe and Chris. Speaking of which, I'm beginning to wonder where they are. At that age they're always late but..."

"So, they're back on?" Spencer interjected.

"Yes. Actually, they're leaving tomorrow for their cross-country trip, so I suspect they're doing some last minute planning," Paige said.

"Wow," Spencer muttered. "Well I'm sure they'll be here any minute."

Paige leaned toward Spencer and in a hushed voice said, "She only told me today and you and I haven't had a chance to talk." Returning her attention to the group, "Shall we go to our table?"

As they sat down at the table Paige noticed how Mollie seemed to appreciate every detail. She was visibly admiring the flowers and even ran her hand along the silk napkin before placing it on her lap. "This is just so beautiful," Mollie said as she turned to

Paul to see he was already eating a roll he took from the bread basket. "Oh Paul," she giggled as she wiped crumbs from his tuxedo jacket, before holding one of his hands under the table. Paige noticed how effortlessly Mollie slid her hand onto his as she turned back to the table. Spencer tapped her and said, "Isn't it time?"

She was preparing to make her way to the stage when Chloe and Chris arrived. They hurried straight over to Paige and Spencer. Chloe hugged her father and then Paige, whispering, "I'm so sorry we're late. There was terrible traffic."

Chloe was flushed and Chris was looking down sheepishly so Paige sensed the real reason for the delay but she gracefully said, "That's Ok, Honey. You made it in time." Then turning her attention to Chris she said, "You look beautiful Chris. Thank you for coming."

"My pleasure Mrs. Michaels. Thank you for having me."

Paige quickly introduced the girls to Mollie and Paul and then Chloe gave Gwen a hug. "You two are the most gorgeous couple here," Gwen whispered. Then raising her voice, "Damn these young gals with their fabulous hair and glowing skin, or should I say after-glow skin!" Paige shook her head as everyone else laughed. The girls sat down, but not before Chris whispered to Chloe, "This is what we get for being late."

"Ok, I think I should get the event going," Paige said before making her way to the podium.

The noise quieted and all eyes turned to the stage as Paige began to speak. "Good evening everyone, and thank you for coming. Like many of you, I have been personally impacted by breast cancer. I lost my mother, Eleanor Michaels, less than two years ago. Tonight we are gathered to raise funds in the hopes that other mothers, daughters, sisters and partners are saved." After the applause, Paige introduced the primary speaker, director of research at a leading cancer institute. Twenty minutes later Paige returned to the stage. "Thank you all for your attention. Now, let's enjoy a wonderful meal and an evening of dancing with friends. The results of the silent auction will be revealed during dessert, so please, there is still plenty of time to bid."

When Paige returned to the table everyone told her what a wonderful job she had done. Spencer turned to her and said, "Your mother would have been impressed."

"Thank you."

Just then their salads were served, followed by an exquisite beef wellington. The talking at their table never ceased, not for a moment. Paige and Mollie spoke about art, Paul and Spencer talked about world events, Gwen offered Chloe and Chris travel tips and in between their side conversations the entire table joked about funny things that have happened to them over the years. It was the most joyful table in the entire ballroom.

After Redmond told a raucous story about getting lost on the subway system and ending up in the wrong borough, the conversation shifted to how much fun living in New York was. Paul said, "There are so many cool things to do. There's just so much available. Today Mollie and I saw a Hitchcock double feature. You can't see those on the big screen everywhere."

"Did you see *Psycho*?" Chris asked. "Chloe wrote a term paper on *Psycho* last year."

Chloe blushed and rubbed her arm against Chris' shoulder.

"No, we saw *Vertigo* and *Marnie*," Paul responded.

"Did you like them?" Paige asked, directing her attention to Mollie.

"Well I had seen *Vertigo* before and it's a great film but I thought *Marnie* was particularly weird and even a bit bleak."

"*Marnie* is one of Gwen's favorite films, isn't that right?" Paige asked.

Gwen nodded.

"It's such a dark film, it doesn't seem like something you'd like," Mollie said, quizzically.

"Oh I think it's wonderful, trying to unravel who that woman is and where she comes from."

"Gwen has always had a fascination with women of mystery, being one herself," Redmond added.

"It's been years since I've seen it but if I recall, it's really about a woman who hasn't come to terms with past trauma, isn't that right?" Paige asked.

"Exactly," Mollie replied.

"Hmm," Paige muttered, lost in thoughts of her mother. But when she noticed everyone was looking at her she blinked instinctively and Gwen chimed in with, "Of course *Marnie* also has all of that red which is just marvelous. It's my signature color."

Everyone laughed and the conversation moved on. Soon the waiters removed the dinner plates, the band began playing show tunes, and people started heading to the dance floor. Spencer left for the bar to catch up with a business associate and Redmond offered to join him. Chris asked Chloe to dance and Paul followed suit, escorting Mollie to the dance floor. Left alone, Paige and Gwen finally had a chance to speak.

"So, how are you doing?" Paige asked.

"Oh, I'm wonderful darling, just wonderful."

Confused, Paige contemplated what to say when Gwen continued, "When Redmond called from the airport and told me to put on my dancing shoes, all of my anxiety disappeared. Paige, I can't tell you, it was like there had been a vise around my neck and I was finally released. So tonight is a celebration, like a rebirth or something but with diamonds."

"So, Redmond said things went well?" Paige probed.

"Well it's obvious darling. You should have seen him come into the door. That sad, beaten man he's been lately, well that man was gone and my Redmond came home, beaming and telling me he was ready for a night out on the town. I'm so glad he's finally himself again. Haven't you noticed how animated he is tonight? It's just wonderful."

Paige smiled ever so slightly but couldn't avoid blinking. Gwen, who now looked curious, was about to say something when Spencer and Redmond returned.

"So my lady, shall we?" Redmond asked, holding his hand out to Gwen.

"Well you'll have to excuse me, I'm doing to dance with this fabulous man," Gwen said as she took Redmond's hand and followed him to the dance floor.

"Well," Spencer said reaching out his arm, "Should we give it a whirl?"

Paige nodded.

As they arrived on the dance floor, Spencer put one arm around Paige's waist and the other on her shoulder and gazed into her eyes. *He looks happy*, she thought.

Paige looked over to see Gwen and Redmond spinning around the dance floor like there was no tomorrow but Paige knew that come midnight her glass slippers would be shattered.

"Spencer, I'm worried about Gwen and Redmond. He didn't tell her. She thinks you made some kind of miracle deal. She doesn't know."

Spencer sighed. "Maybe he didn't want to ruin her night. I'm sure he'll tell her later or tomorrow. Maybe he just needed to loosen up first. He had a pretty stiff drink when we were at the bar."

Paige's heart sank. She turned again to look at Gwen, but Gwen couldn't see anyone except for the man she loved, twirling her around.

Then Paige turned to see Mollie and Paul dancing, holding each other as if no one else was in the room. To her own surprise, Paige laughed.

"Ok, what could possibly be funny?" Spencer asked.

"Mollie and I saw Renoir's dancing couples at The MET and it just occurred to me that now, the six of us, we're like those couples. I wonder if Mollie noticed."

Spencer smiled. "I think she and Paul are too busy staring at each other."

Paige tried to catch Mollie's eye but her eyes were locked onto Paul and she couldn't catch her attention. "They may be the luckiest people here," Paige said.

"People make their own luck, remember? At least those who can."

She smiled.

Spencer spun Paige around until she laughed again and then he said, "You know Gwen and Redmond, they'll have to sort this out themselves. Everyone has to sort out their own life."

"I know."

An hour later the silent auction results were announced. Spencer won the wine he bid on. Everyone at their table congratulated him and soon they were all hugging each other and saying goodnight. "Marvelous event, darling. Bravo," Gwen said as she hugged Paige. Then, as if on his honeymoon, Redmond put his arm out and said, "Come on my love." Gwen took his hand as Paige watched them saunter off, wondering if she would ever see Gwen so happy again.

CHAPTER 10

The next morning Kayla Washington awoke to pounding on her apartment door. She groggily took her "sweet dreams" eye mask off, looked at her clock and wondered who was banging on her door on a Sunday morning. "Hold on," she hollered, as she slipped on her robe and stumbled to her front door.

"Kay-Kay, open the door!" she heard.

"Leala, is that you?" Kay-Kay called as she unlocked the door. "Girl, your place better be on fire waking me up when you know I'm jetlagged," Kay-Kay said as she made her way to her living room couch, Leala following behind, with a stack of newspapers under her arm. Kay-Kay plopped down on her overstuffed yellow couch with Leala standing before her, nearly hyperventilating. "Shit, your place isn't on fire for real is it?" Kay-Kay asked.

"It's the store..." Leala said, but before she could explain Kay-Kay jumped in, "The store, what about the store? I knew I shouldn't have left you to take care of things for the week. You better tell me what's wrong."

"Nothing's wrong. Why haven't you answered your phone? Have you even seen the paper? Damn, Kay-Kay, why didn't you tell me what was going on?"

"Do I have to get a translator or are you gonna tell me what you're talking about?"

"You don't know? You don't know! Oh my god, Kay-Kay..."

Kay-Kay started shaking her head, "Lea, Spill it or I'm going back to sleep and pretending this was a dream."

"You're famous! There are reporters outside of the store taking pictures and, and, well check your phone. I left you a million messages. Probably everyone you know called and..."

"Slow down, Lea. I silenced my phone to get some shut eye. I'm still on West Coast time," Kay-Kay said as she grabbed her cellphone off the coffee table and looked to discover her mailbox was filled. Before she could listen to them or read her many new

143

emails Leala said, "Here, just look," as she handed her the stack of newspapers.

Kay-Kay just sat there with the newspapers on her lap, "What's going on? You sure Jay didn't slip you something, you're talking crazy. And shouldn't you be at the store doing inventory?"

"Page 6, open to page 6," Leala said as she walked into the kitchenette to get a glass of water to try to calm herself.

Kay-Kay opened the first newspaper and there it was, a photograph of Caroline Kennedy wearing a Kayla Washington original. She truly couldn't believe it, and even blinked and rubbed at her eyes, sure she was hallucinating. When the image remained she blurted, "I dressed a Kennedy?!? Caroline Kennedy wore my dress!"

"Forget Caroline Kennedy, Gayle King, you know as in Oprah's BFF, she wore one too," Leala revealed.

Leala returned to the living room and sat on a chair kitty-corner to Kay-Kay who was frantically searching the other newspapers where she saw more pictures of Caroline Kennedy in her gown as well as Diane Sawyer, Gayle King and Paige Michaels. "I don't believe it!" she exclaimed.

"When you were in LA I got an order over the phone for four of our best gowns, you know the hand-beaded expensive ones on those fabrics you got on your last trip. A messenger picked them up. I had no idea. I assumed it was a fancy wedding or something."

"Shit, why didn't you mention it when I checked in with you?"

"I wanted to surprise you when you got back. I thought you'd be impressed with how much I sold," Leala explained.

"I just don't believe it," Kay-Kay said.

"You've gotta get yourself together and down to the store."

Kay-Kay sat perfectly still, staring at the last photo. "I don't believe it," she repeated.

Leala snapped her fingers and said, "Well believe it. You've gotta get to the store Kay-Kay, like now, it's cray-cray."

Kay-Kay looked up at her and then noticed a small envelope in Leala's hand. "What's that?" she asked.

"Oh, sorry. I was so caught up. This was outside your door when I got here." She handed Kay-Kay the envelope. As soon as she opened it she took a deep breath. Enclosed was a note on personalized stationery bearing Paige's name, address and telephone number.

"Dear Kay-Kay,

Your talent, bravery and tenacity never cease to amaze me. Your designs are so beautiful! I was honored to wear your dress. Thank you. Congratulations on all of your much deserved success. I hope it's all right that I am reaching out now, you've been on my mind. Kay-Kay, I should never have let our friendship go and I owe you a long overdue apology. Our friendship meant more to me than my actions suggest and it was inexcusable to walk away without even discussing it, and for that I am deeply sorry. I hope we will have the chance to reconnect. I have two friends you would just love; they remind me so much of you. I hope your mother and brother are well. Congratulations again on realizing your dream.

With love and regret,
Your friend,
Paige"

Kay-Kay folded the note over, held it in her hands and smiled. Leala looked like she was about to say something when Kay-Kay jumped up and said, "Ok, I'll get in the shower, you make some coffee. It's going to be a big day."

*

"What the hell is that?" Jake asked, as he opened his eyes.
    "Go back to sleep."

He sat up to find Jen wrapped in the blanket, her long blonde hair covering her back. "Hey, you took all the blanket again," he said, yanking some of it playfully from her.

"I woke up a while ago and I was bored."

"What are you watching?" he asked, looking at the television in disbelief.

"It's the *E True Hollywood Story of the Kardashians* and I don't want to hear a word from you after the crap you make me watch."

He shook his head and leaned back down to try to go back to sleep when he heard an E-News report interrupt a commercial. "Turn that up," he said as he sat up and leaned forward.

There was Paige being interviewed by Giuliana Rancic, saying, "It's a Kayla Washington design," and looking even more beautiful than she did when she was a teenager.

He heard Giuliana reply, "Well that must be at least the third I've heard that name tonight. I think it's safe to say there is a hot new designer on the scene. Thank you so much for stopping to chat with us and for all of your good work." He saw Spencer standing beside Paige, and looking at her with pride, like he too had always done.

Jake started smiling wider than he ever had, shaking his head and muttering, "I don't believe it."

"What?" Jen asked.

"It's nothing," he said.

"What is it? Tell me?"

"Sometimes you think you messed up so badly that it can't ever be made right."

"And?" she pressed.

"And it's been a long time since someone surprised me in a good way. I didn't know if that could still happen."

"Uh, well I bet I can surprise you," she said, as she grabbed a pillow and started hitting him with it.

"Oh, you gonna be like that now! Well, now you're in trouble," he said as he grabbed the pillow from her and starting hitting back until she lay down laughing hysterically and begging him to stop. He leaned over and said, "Mercy, you want mercy now?"

*

As Paige observed Chloe and Chris holding hands and making eyes at each other she thought about Jake and how different it was for them. She knew the time had come to face it all with Spencer. Her heart was racing. *What should I say; that he was a boy I once loved and he broke my heart? Should I tell him about Kay-Kay? He knows how devastated I had been about my father, but what about my mother? I have to tell him what I learned about my mother.*

"Do you have your car cellphone charger?" Spencer asked.

"Yes. Don't worry, I have everything for the millionth time," Chloe insisted before hugging him again. "I'll bring these down," he said as picked up two duffel bags.

"I'll go with you," Chris said, before turning to Paige and saying, "Thanks again for everything Mrs. Michaels."

Paige smiled, thinking how these final moments all seemed to be happening in slow motion and were a garbled mix of the words said aloud and those she was thinking. *I can't believe Chloe is leaving. When I left for school I was in so much pain. What a relief she's so happy.*

As Chris walked out Chloe turned to face her mother.

"I just can't believe this moment is here," Paige said.

"Awe, you're not going to cry are you?"

"I just may," Paige said, before leaning in to hug her again. *Oh sweet girl, this is so hard* she thought.

"Thank you for letting me go," Chloe whispered. "You don't have to worry. I'm really happy."

Paige nodded, still hugging her. "There's so much ahead of you. Be open to it all. Don't waste a moment. And be kind to each other, you and Chris. No matter what happens, respect yourself and each other." *Don't make my mistakes.*

Chloe pulled away and said, "I'll try."

"And you know your Dad and I are only a phone call away. We can come to you, wherever you are, any time you need us and you can always come back, no questions asked."

"Uh, yeah right. No questions?"

"Well, you can always come back, smart one," Paige said sarcastically.

"I know, Mom. I really need to go, Chris is waiting."

I hope the laughter doesn't leave with her. Will it be silent, that deafening silence? I can't live locked in a frame like my mother. There has to be another way to feel safe.

"Chloe you have to be cautious too. Please don't forget all I have taught you. The world isn't always…"

"Safe. I know, Mom. Chris does too. We'll be fine," Chloe interjected.

Just then Spencer returned. "Well, everything is packed up and I plugged your first stop into the GPS."

Chloe shook her head, "We'll be fine, Dad, but thanks."

He's such a good man, Paige thought.

"Ok, well Chris is in the car so, I guess it's time," Spencer said.

This is it, Paige thought. *Chloe is leaving. She's really leaving. God, she looks so happy. She's at the beginning.* Jake again came to her mind. *He broke my heart and I hadn't seen him in decades, not until Dad's funeral. I wasn't myself. I was completely numb and I guess I wanted to feel something. It's indefensible and I don't know how I ever could have hurt Spencer. Will it cost me everything?*

Chloe hugged her father one more time and then her mother. As she picked up her backpack and turned to leave, everything Paige wanted to say to Spencer coursed through her mind. *I love you, who you really are and I know you love me too. We're not perfect, Spencer. Our lives had become so patterned and you seemed distant for a long time. I think there was a growing gap between who we were and who we became. I know I fell into the gap and it's inexcusable. I have lived in this resounding silence because you needed it, and perhaps because I am a coward in some ways too and it was easier. But no more. I'm so sorry. I love you Spencer. Please tell me you can forgive or at least that you want to. Please tell me we can rebuild. We can't live in silence. I lost myself for a time but I'm back now and I don't want to lose you.*

Her thoughts were interrupted when she saw Chloe walk out the door. She leaned forward and closed the door before taking a deep breath and turning to face Spencer.

ABOUT THE AUTHOR

Patricia Leavy is an independent scholar and novelist, formerly Associate Professor of Sociology and the Founding Director of Gender Studies at Stonehill College in Massachusetts. Leavy has emerged as a leader in the qualitative and arts-based research communities. She is the author of the acclaimed novel, *Low-Fat Love* (Sense Publishers, 2011) which has inspired a radio show and blog. She is the author of numerous non-fiction works including *Fiction as Research Practice* (Left Coast Press, 2013); *Transdisciplinary Research Practice: Issue and Problem-Centered Approaches to Research* (Left Coast Press, 2011); *Oral History: Understanding Qualitative Research* (Oxford University Press, 2011); *Method Meets Art: Arts-Based Research Practice* (Guilford Press, 2009); and *Iconic Events: Media, Politics and Power in Retelling History* (Lexington Books, 2007). She is coauthor of *The Practice of Qualitative Research* (Sage Publications, 2005, 2011) and *Feminist Research Practice: A Primer* (Sage, 2007). She is the editor of *The Oxford Handbook of Qualitative Research* (Oxford University Press, forthcoming) and the co-editor of *Hybrid Identities: Theoretical and Empirical Examinations* (Haymarket, 2008); *Handbook of Emergent Methods* (Guilford Press, 2008); *Emergent Methods in Social Research* (Sage, 2006) and *Approaches to Qualitative Research* (Oxford University Press, 2004). In addition to serving as the editor for the *Social Fictions, Teaching Gender* and *Teaching Race & Ethnicity* book series with Sense Publishers, she is also the editor for the Oxford University Press book series *Understanding Qualitative Research*. She is regularly quoted by the national media for her expertise on popular culture, gender and other sociological topics and has appeared on television programs including "The Glenn Beck Show" and "Lou Dobbs Tonight." The New England Sociological Association named Leavy the 2010 "Sociologist of the Year." She offers book talks as well as keynotes and workshops on a variety of topics. Please visit www.patricialeavy.com for more information.

CPSIA information can be obtained at www.ICGtesting.com
Printed in the USA
BVOW09s1038201214

380038BV00004B/35/P

9 789462 092853